Elements of
WITCHCRAFT

About the Author

Ellen Dugan, also known as the Garden Witch, is a psychic-clairvoy-
ant who lives in Missouri with her husband and three teenage children. A practicing Witch for seventeen years, look for other articles
by Ellen in Llewellyn's annual *Witchy Day Planner*, *Magical Almanac*,
Wicca Almanac, and *Herbal Almanac*.

Elements of
WITCHCRAFT

Natural Magick for Teens

ELLEN DUGAN

2003
Llewellyn Publications
St. Paul, Minnesota 55164-0383, U.S.A.

FIRST EDITION
First Printing, 2003

Book design and editing by Rebecca Zins
Cover design by Kevin R. Brown
Cover images © Digital Vision
Interior illustrations by Kerigwen

Library of Congress Cataloging-in-Publication Data
Dugan, Ellen, 1963-
    Elements of witchcraft : natural magick for teens / Ellen Dugan.—1st ed.
        p.   cm.
    Includes bibliographical references and index.
    ISBN 0-7387-0393-1
    1. Witchcraft.   2. Teenagers—Miscellanea.   I. Title.

    BF1571.5.T44D86 2003
    133.4'3—dc21

                                                    2003040081

Llewellyn Worldwide does not participate in, endorse, or have any authority or responsibility concerning private business transactions between our authors and the public.

All mail addressed to the author is forwarded but the publisher cannot, unless specifically instructed by the author, give out an address or phone number.

Any Internet references contained in this work are current at publication time, but the publisher cannot guarantee that a specific location will continue to be maintained. Please refer to the publisher's website for links to authors' websites and other sources.

Llewellyn Publications
A Division of Llewellyn Worldwide, Ltd.
P.O. Box 64383, Dept. 0-7387-0393-1
St. Paul, MN 55164-0383, U.S.A.
www.llewellyn.com

Printed in the United States of America on recycled paper

Other Books by Ellen Dugan

Garden Witchery: Magick from the Ground Up

Contents

II
The Elements of Nature

3 • The Element of Earth . . . 41

4 • The Element of Air . . . 61

III
Looking Deeper into Natural Magick

IV
Walking the Path
of Natural Magick

12 • A Natural Witch . . . 219

ACKNOWLEDGMENTS

First and foremost, a big thank-you goes to Megan Atwood, who initially asked me if I would be interested in writing a book for teens. Thanks, Megan, for believing in me, and for all of your enthusiasm and support. Thanks also to Kerigwen for the knockout illustrations; to my editor, Becky Zins, who always makes the editing process a fun and exciting one; and to publicists Jill Johansen and Lisa Braun.

To the wise and witchy women and magickal men that I am privileged to call friends—Cindy, Paula, Amanda, Nicole, Amy, Scott, Colleen, Dan, and Mickie—who all reminded me, each in their own way, to remain true to myself and to what I had to say, both as a Witch and as a mom. Thanks, guys, for the support and hand-holding when I fretted and worried, and for your enthusiasm for the topic and indulgence with me when I was on a roll. Also, I'd like to express my appreciation to "Auntie Dorothy," a.k.a. Dorothy Morrison, for her straight talk, humor, friendship, and savvy advice.

To the magickal young friends that have come unexpectedly into my life: Noire, Willow, Chelsea, Jake, and especially Brittany. Thanks for allowing me to "pick your brains." I feel very fortunate to count all of you among my friends.

For my two sons and to my daughter, thanks for being all-around wonderful teenage kids, and for cheering me on from the beginning, reading and critiquing my drafts and making excellent suggestions. I love all three of you for being the individuals that you are.

Finally, to the handsome young man who asked me to marry him some twenty-two years ago, when I was still a teen myself. One crisp fall night, I looked him straight in the eye, told him the truth about my talents and prepared to lose him. To my amazement, he didn't even flinch.

I stood there and tried to explain to him just how different his life would be. What about any kids that we might have? What if they all took after me and were naturally psychic or clairvoyant? Then he'd be outnumbered. Could he handle being the father of kids who could do things like I could? He tried to assure me that he could.

"Just wait until they're all in their teens," I warned him.

As I rambled on, he silenced me with a kiss. He looked down into my eyes and replied softly, "I know what you're trying to tell me, babe. You're a Witch."

I held my breath and waited.

"So what?" He grinned at me and pulled me close. "It should make life pretty interesting."

What a guy. I am happy to report that after twenty-one years of marriage and now three teenage kids to boot . . . I am quite certain that I have managed to make his life very interesting indeed.

INTRODUCTION
A Day in the Life of a Teen Witch

As the full moon begins to rise unseen in the eastern sky, a fourteen-year-old girl stands alone under the barren trees in her backyard. It is a cold February night and an ice storm has been forecast for the area. She glances to the leaden sky and shivers. The girl draws her coat closer around her as she calls out for her lost black kitten, again. *How did Jasmine manage to sneak out?* she wonders for the millionth time.

It's been a couple of hours since the family discovered that their kitten was missing, and it is getting colder. Some of the neighbors even tried to help. Armed with flashlights and bundled up against the cold, they searched the neighborhood, but with no success. Both of her older brothers are still out driving around and looking, hoping to find the small cat. How in the world will they ever find a little black cat in the dark?

Worried and tearful, the girl asks herself if there is anything else she could possibly do to help. Then she stops and considers. Of course there is something else she can do, she realizes proudly. After all . . . she is a Witch.

She tosses her waist-length hair behind her, wipes her eyes, and stands up straight and tall. "Goddess, do you hear me?" she asks quietly.

As if in answer, the wind rises and shakes the branches of the trees above her head. The Goddess is listening, the young Witch realizes, and always has been. *All right then,* she decides. *It's time to get to work.* The girl pushes her wind-tangled hair out of her face and raises her hands, palms up and out to her sides. She slows her breathing and closes her eyes as the cold wind swirls around her. She takes a deep breath and centers herself as she silently calls on the Goddess to send Jasmine safely home.

For a moment, the wind dies and a stillness falls over the winter garden. With her eyes slowly opening, a tremulous smile spreads over the girl's face. "Thanks for listening," the young Witch whispers. Then, with renewed force, the storm winds rush through the yard again.

From the front of the house, the sounds of her two brothers arriving home carries to her clearly in the wintry night air. As if on cue, an ice pellet bounces off of the frozen ground, then another. A moment later, familiar footsteps sound from behind the girl and a warm arm drapes over her shoulders. The girl turns to look at her mother as her mother urges her to come inside.

"Mom," the young Witch says with a determined look in her eye, "I've got an idea."

Once inside, the girl heads to the magickal cabinet in her mother's room. There she takes out a favored picture of the Egyptian cat goddess Bast. She sets this picture of Bast and a photo of Jasmine together on the top of the cabinet. Her mother places a small pink votive candle into a holder and steps back as her daughter lights the candle. The girl then sets the candleholder on top of the photo of her pet and improvises a quick invocation to the goddess Bast.

"Bast, I call on you—send my kitten home to me, and as I will it, then so shall it be."

As the candle begins to burn, the young Witch envisions her pet on a long silver leash. In her mind's eye, the girl gently gathers in the leash as the kitten trots home to her. The girl then calls on the strength of the storm to speed the little cat back home as quickly as possible. She closes her spell by thanking the Goddess for her help. The spell is cast. Quietly, she leaves the room and goes to watch out the living room windows as rain and pellets of ice begin to fall steadily.

Her father lights a fire in the wood-burning stove as the family begins to face the grim reality of losing their precious pet to the ice storm. The girl is anxious but quiet. Her mother encourages her to have hope. A short time later, a loud knock comes from the front door. It is the next-door neighbor. He thinks the cat may be hiding in his backyard. The family, as one, streams out of the house to go and see. It is the little black cat. She is cold and wet, but fine. The family hustles back inside to their warm house and the girl wraps up her sneaky kitten in a towel, and then sits with her pet by the fire, gently rubbing Jasmine dry.

"That was really fast, Mom," she grins up at her mother as the kitten's happy purrs fill the living room.

"It certainly was," her mother smiles right back.

The girl's older brothers exchange a significant look. They stop arguing for a moment over whether or not to give the kitten any warm milk, and both get up and walk down the hall to look at the remnants of the spell and the candle that is burning in their mother's room.

From the back of the house, one brother calls out, "Who did the spell? Kat or Mom?"

"Your sister did this one," their mother replies.

"Hey, cool," a brother announces.

"How long did that take to work, anyway?" the second brother asks, as they return to the living room.

"About fifteen minutes," their mother informs them.

As the girl's family discusses their kitten's latest escapade, and the debate once again ensues over what is best for Jasmine to eat, the girl holds her pet and says a quiet thank-you to the Goddess.

Her father listens thoughtfully to his family and then rises to tend the fire. After adding another log to the blaze, he gently nudges his daughter in the ribs with his toe and says with a sparkle in his eyes, "Hey, Kat—next time, do the spell first. It would have saved us from searching out in the cold for two hours."

The young Witch laughs with her father and hugs her pet closer. She catches her mother's eye and they share a knowing grin . . .

Just another average day in the life of a fourteen-year-old Witch.

I

The Nature of Magick

I am SURE
there is MAGIC
in everything.

—FRANCES HODGSON BURNETT

ONE

A Witch's Introduction to Natural Magick

Hello, Teen Witch. So, you've decided you want to learn about Witchcraft and natural magick? Perhaps you've searched the Internet and looked through a book or two on the topic of Witchcraft, and you're curious. I bet that you have lots of questions. *What is magick, anyway?* you may be thinking. *Will a book really help me understand how magick works? More importantly, can I actually become a Witch all by myself?*

The mere title of this book alone may be causing you some confusion and raising even more questions. *Magick is natural? I thought magick was supernatural . . . you know, graveyard dirt, chanting mysterious charms by the dark of the moon, mystical bubbling potions that boil in glowing cauldrons, fighting off supernatural bad guys, that sort of thing.*

Gee, how very mysterious and gothic. That sounds like an episode of *Charmed* to me. Forget all the silliness you have seen on television or read in a trashy book. Would you care for a little dose of reality instead? I thought you might. Let me start out by answering a few of those questions and addressing those concerns right now.

Magick *is* natural and it is very real. Who could doubt the reality of magick? Magick is as elementary as wishing upon a star, a baby's first laugh, and falling in love. There is magick in a snowstorm and enchantment to be found as you quietly watch the sun set on a balmy summer evening. For magick is in all things at all times.

Natural magick is both a way of life and an art. With natural magick, you don't *use* magick. You simply work with the natural energies of the Earth that are already swirling around you. Yes, that's right, the natural energies of the Earth. The physical world is made up of four basic, natural elements; these are earth, air, fire, and water. It is these four magickal elements that a Witch will tap into. Magickal energy can be found in *everything* in nature, such as plants, rocks, and crystals. There is enchantment to be discovered in the towering trees and colorful, scented flowers. There are also lessons to be learned from the waters of the lakes and the mighty rivers.

Guess what that means? That means we are going to be working outside quite often. Natural magick will require you to get up and go outdoors. Why, you may ask? Well, because outside is generally where nature is. If you are outdoors and you close your eyes in delight as you feel the breeze streaming through your hair and lifting your spirits, you can embrace firsthand the idea of air being a magickal element of change.

This experience is much more profound for you as a novice Witch than if you try to imagine that breeze indoors, cooped up in your room. Go outside and get your hands dirty! Feel the soil beneath your fingers. Plant some flowers in your yard or in a container. Water your new plant and take care of it. See what your plant friend has to teach you. Dangle your toes in a pond or lake on a hot summer's day. Run around outside and try to catch falling leaves before they hit the ground on a crisp fall afternoon. Experiencing nature in all her glory will help you learn to first sense and then to work with the magickal powers of nature.

Let's head outdoors for a moment. Look around you and answer these questions. What do you see and feel? Is the sun or the moon in the sky above you? Is it hot or cold, wet or dry outside? Do you live in the city, in the suburbs, or on a farm? Are you living in the desert, the mountains, or the plains? Do you live near the woods or by a river? Are you alongside a lake or perched at the seashore? What sorts of animals are native to your area? What kinds of birds show up at the backyard bird feeder?

How do the seasons inspire you where you live? Do you have bitter cold winters with snow or do you have mild winters and rain? A breeze could be blowing past you. What scents are carried along with it? What sounds do you hear? Wind chimes, or perhaps the sounds of the neighbor's dog barking? Do you hear birdsong? What kind of bird is it? Is it a cardinal or the squawk of a blue jay? Did you know that blue jays symbolize tenacity? To see blue jays flying around you is a sign to be a little more assertive and to stand your ground.

Natural magick is a process in which you tune into the rhythms, the tides, and the energies of the seasons, the elements, and nature. That's why I fired so many questions at you right off the bat—to make you more aware of your natural surroundings and how they can magickally affect your life. Get all your five-plus senses involved. Start paying closer attention to the signs of nature. You'll most likely be amazed at what they have to teach you.

As you begin to learn natural magick, you will work with the tides of the seasons and in harmony with the four elements. Natural magick is usually performed in a practical, quiet, and low-profile way, just as the young Witch performed her spell in the Introduction.

The story in the Introduction was true, not a work of fiction. That was a prime example of a Teen Witch working with a belief in the Goddess, the magick of nature, and the love for her pet. She called on the natural powers of the ice storm and then focused on the element of fire, symbolized by the candle flame. She combined all of these components into a spell to bring about her desired result, the return of her kitten. How well do I know this Teen Witch? Very well—the girl in the Introduction is my daughter.

How did my daughter learn magick? Well, she learned it from me. I am a Witch myself. As of this writing, I have been a practicing Witch for about seventeen years. How did I learn magick? Well, the truth is that I taught myself. I don't claim to be secretly trained by a long-dead family member. There are no long-lost magickal relatives hiding in my family tree, just Irish, Danish, and German ancestors. That's right, I read books and researched Witchcraft and the religion of Wicca all on my own. I talked to other Witches, memorized my basics, and made my own decisions about what variety of magick I liked. For me, that was herbalism (the use of herbs and plants in magick) and natural magick. I worked hard and practiced my butt off . . . just as you're going to do.

The Tradition of Witchcraft

Many teens, and adults for that matter, wonder where Witchcraft really comes from. Was all this fabulous occult information hiding some-where in a secret magickal library over in England or somewhere? Who discovered it? How did it all begin? What are its origins? Well, probably the truest answer that I can give you is that Witchcraft is a tradition.

Modern Witchcraft, or Wicca, is based on the older folk wisdom or tradition of innocent spells, herb and moon lore, divination techniques, and ways of natural healing. This ancient tradition was handed down orally throughout the years from mother to daughter and father to son. In the Middle Ages, very few people could read or write, let alone had access to books. So what we know of the older traditions of Witchcraft has been transformed into country charms, weather lore, legends, and folktales. The keepers of this legacy were the wisewomen and the cun-ning men. They were the midwives, healers, and the wise folk of their communities or villages.

"Wicca" is an Anglo-Saxon word that has several meanings, the first being from the root word *wicce*, which means "wise." (Get it . . . wise-women.) To be a Wiccan is to be one of the Wise Ones. Some other folks will point out that the word also means "to shape or to bend," and either definition is correct. You bend reality with your magick and shape the future to your wishes. In modern times, the word "Wicca" is the name for the religion of the Witch.

Wicca also incorporates the mythologies and traditions of numer-ous other cultures as well. This includes a smattering of various old earth religions, such as the ancient Norse and Celtic mythologies and beliefs. Wiccans hold to the theory, as did many ancient cultures before us, that the land is sacred and that the Earth is a holy place. Wicca is a polytheistic religion, meaning we believe in the existence of more than one God. Our religion is based on the belief of a God and a Goddess.

These feminine and masculine energies are two parts of a whole, just as in nature. You can't have one without the other.

The God and the Goddess —Who Are They?

Okay, so who are this Goddess and God that I have been referring to? They are the basis of the religion of Wicca. Witchcraft, which is a part of Wicca, is a religious thing—so is life. Recently one of my teenage nephews approached me and nervously began to ask me questions about Witchcraft and God.

"Aunt Ellen, I have a friend who is interested in Wicca," he began. "Now I know that you aren't evil or anything . . . but in my youth Bible class, they taught us that Witchcraft is wrong." He smiled nervously at me and waited to hear my reply.

"Why did they say that it's wrong?" I asked him.

He shuffled his feet and looked down at the ground. "Well, they keep warning us to stay away from it, like it's going to get us or something. You know, the whole devil thing."

"Witches don't believe in the devil. And we certainly don't work with him," I answered him firmly, and watched to see what his reaction would be.

His face lit up. "Really? You know, I thought that you said something to me before about a Goddess or God. You believe in God, right?"

"Yes, I do. Witches believe in a God and a Goddess. I think of them as two equal halves of the whole—a masculine and a feminine side of divinity."

"So how come you don't go to church with us?" he asked me.

"This is my church," I told him, gesturing beyond the backyard where we were standing. "For Witches, nature is sacred."

"Oh, you mean Witchcraft is all about nature?"

"Yes," I explained. "It is about seeing the divine in everything. Being a Witch means that you work hard to be a good, moral, and ethical person. I know that the God and the Goddess are watching over me, and they help me out when I ask them to."

"Okay, I get it." He thought about that for a moment, plainly relieved. He looked at me, slung his arm around my shoulder, and gave me a hug. "So, who is this God and Goddess of yours? Tell me about them."

To many ancient cultures, the Goddess was a symbol of the oceans, the earth, and the moon. The Goddess was directly responsible for not only the fertility of the land, but the animals and the people as well. The God was her other half and consort. He was often represented as the sun that brightened the sky and brought life to the land. We have known the God and Goddess by many different names for centuries. Here are just a few you are probably familiar with.

To the ancient Greeks, they were known as Helios the sun god and Selene the moon goddess. The Romans called the god of the sun Apollo, and his twin sister was Diana, the goddess of the moon. To the indigenous people of America, they are Earth Mother and Sky Father. See what I mean about that nature theme? The truth is that you can call them by any name you wish. Go with whatever you're most comfortable with: God and Goddess, Lord and Lady, Earth Mother and Sky Father, or Goddess of the moon and God of the sun.

It is important to know that we do not worship the moon and the sun; they are merely natural symbols or representations of the Goddess and the God. We see them as kind and loving deities, similar to a mother and a father. They watch over us, advise us, and help us through the tough times. They also expect the best out of us personally, like real parents.

The easiest way to get to know the God and Goddess is through meditation. Meditation isn't difficult to learn. Basically you find a quiet, safe spot in nature or at home, and settle in and get comfy. Ideally, this should be someplace where you will not be disturbed for a short time. Relax, take a few deep, cleansing breaths, and clear your mind. Now imagine yourself somewhere in nature. When I prepare to meditate, I like to imagine myself walking into a secret garden. Try this and see how it works for you.

Visualize or imagine yourself standing at the base of ten stone steps. As you begin to climb up, step by step, count silently backwards from ten to one. When you count back to the number one, you have reached the top of the steps. Now, see before you an ivy-covered garden gate. Open the gate and imagine you are entering a secret garden. Once you are in the secret garden, let your imagination go and your subconscious can take over. At this point of the meditation you could ask to meet the God and Goddess; let your mind drift and use your imagination. See where this leads you and what they have to say.

When you feel that you're ready to end the meditation, go back to the garden entrance, step out and close the gate behind you. Now count down those ten garden steps as you descend them, starting at the top with number one. When you reach step number ten, take a deep breath, blow it out, and open your eyes. Take a moment and jot down your impressions. What did you see and hear? What did you learn? How did that make you feel?

Another type of meditation used by Witches is called "pathworking." Pathworking is a guided meditation and this is sort of like going on an imaginary trip. With a guided meditation, you follow a story line that leads you through a lesson. This story teaches you a magickal lesson or introduces you to a nature spirit or even a deity. There are several guided meditations in this book. Some of these will direct you through the lesson from beginning to end, while others allow you to follow your own mind's imaginary path.

Whether you use meditation or simply sit on the grass and pray, take the time to introduce yourself to the Lord and Lady; they are waiting for you. The God and Goddess are real and they are a fundamental part of Witchcraft and magick. And if you call on them, they will hear you.

How Do I Get Started?

If you want to be a Witch and practice natural magick, you are probably going to have to learn your craft the hard way, just like I did— through study, experimentation, trial and error, and on your own. But you know what? Your solitary training can be every bit as effective and true as those who claim a formal type of training. And don't you ever let anyone tell you differently.

How do you start your own training, you may wonder? There may be so many questions buzzing around inside of your head that it makes it hard to know exactly where to begin. So, let's kick this off with something simple: a little healing exercise for you to try your hand at, and an introduction into natural magick.

A healing spell for yourself might involve taking an early morning barefoot stroll in the backyard (pick a nice day for this), a little meditating, and then sitting on the dewy grass to watch the sunrise. Surprised? Don't be. Natural magick works in harmony with the laws of nature.

Dawn Healing Ritual

As the first rays of the sun brighten up the eastern sky, place your hands on the ground. Feel the dew and the grass beneath your fingers. Then close your eyes and imagine the stabilizing influence of the earth and the cleansing properties of the water are giving you strength and helping to wash away any sadness or illness that you carry. Open your eyes and tip up your head to watch the sunrise. Feel the breeze stir your hair and the strength of the sun begin to wash over you. Make a quiet request to the Lord and Lady. Ask for their help in starting a new day with energy and health and to put old, hurtful feelings behind you. Settle in and feel the peace and possibilities of a new day and of new beginnings slide over you. Take a deep breath in, hold it for a few seconds, and now blow it out.

There, your first ritual. Simple, quiet, and easy. What? You were expecting thunder and lightning as the wind whipped around your celestial robes? I sure hope you aren't standing under any big trees. That's a great way to get your butt fried by lightning. Do you want the truth about magick, or fiction? The truth, then.

True magick and Witchcraft are not all about the Hollywood power image. Wicca is a legally recognized religion here in the United States. Real Witches do not, as a matter of course, battle demons and supernatural bad guys. That's just TV make-believe. We actually do not believe in demons or worship them in any way.

The truth is that once you tune yourself in to the natural world, and begin to recognize the subtle energy of nature, magickal energy can be found all around you. For teens who are interested in the Craft, natural magick is a respectable way to start your studies. So let's warm up the single most important tool that is ever used in Witchcraft. Can you guess what that tool might be? That very important tool is your mind.

The Most Powerful Tool in Magick

Before we begin to perform any other magick, we must first understand what natural magick truly is. Magick is the art and science of effecting positive change in your life. You may attain this change by your will or desire to make these personal improvements and by working in harmony with nature. The only way you can really change your life is to change yourself. So, then, with natural magick, you will work on becoming an improved and healthier person, as well as a strong, kind, and wise Witch. If you are looking to change your life for the better, natural magick could be a good place for you to begin.

Natural magick is gentle and calm. You don't control or force others or the elements. Magick happens when you combine the natural energies from the four elements, empower them with your love, and then send them out with the knowledge that positive change will happen. A fine example is what my daughter accomplished with her "come home kitten" spell in the Introduction.

Now, flip back a page and take another look at the dawn healing ritual. It was easy, elegant, and basic. However, don't underestimate it because it is uncomplicated. There were no tools or props involved. Natural magick does not require the use of elaborate ritual tools and accessories. If you think that you would enjoy having a set of magickal tools, that's certainly a fun thing to own, but it's not necessary for natural magick.

You do not require a fancy ritual robe or cape. You do not need to spend a lot of cash to practice magick. Save your money for the important things, like car insurance, your savings account, new clothes, and that nifty stereo system that you have been eyeballing for a while. The accessories you will need, however, are amazingly simple. You will need a generous and loving heart, an open and flexible mind, and the willingness to study and to learn.

Only you, divinity, your imagination, and a call to the elements were required for our dawn healing ritual. By using your powers of visualization, you were calling on the four elements and tapping into their strengths. There was earth for stability, water for cleansing, and air to refresh and revitalize you. The element of fire was represented by the sun's rays to energize you and to get you moving! You have called on the God and Goddess and made a request for health. That has all the elements of a serious magickal working, all in about a quarter of an hour's time. Not too shabby.

The Basics of Magick

Personal Power

Magick begins with you, with your personal power or the force of your own personality. You know what personal power is. It's the physical energy that comes from your body when you feel happy and healthy. Your energy is high when you're cheering your team at a football game, kissing your boyfriend/girlfriend, or laughing and hanging out with your buddies. (Yes, I realize those three things may all happen at the same time. I'm making a point—work with me here.)

If you're at school, at work, or listening to a friend, you are probably in the medium range of personal power. If you are spending time watching TV or a movie, then you are somewhere in the medium-to-low area of personal power. By that I mean you are relaxed and at ease. Your personal energy is low when you're tired, down in the dumps, or not feeling well. Following me so far?

Your personal power shimmers around you all of the time. This power can be perceived as your aura. The aura is a combination of the human spirit and your physical energy that emanates from your body. This energy field can be sensed and seen as a shimmer of heat, or even as a halo of colored light around the entire body.

The aura can be seen and even photographed with special film. This energy surrounds every living thing in nature, such as plants, animals, and people. Your personal power and your aura fluctuate throughout the day, depending on your mood and activity level. In other words, your aura changes as you do.

The differences of your energy can be distinguished by the depth of your auric field. When you're really pumping out the energy, then your aura is huge. (You know how some charismatic folks just seem to glow?) When you are in an everyday range of power, then the aura is smaller, a foot or two above your skin. When you are tired or ill, the aura sucks in close to your body. All of that energy is focused internally and it hugs you tight.

As for individual magickal power, it comes in all different varieties. If you are an outgoing, vivacious person, your particular magickal energy will be a strong blast of high-powered energy (a big, bright, sparkling aura). If you are quiet and serious, then your magick will be a steady stream of energy, unwavering and solid (an average aura—colorful and strong). If you are shy and timid, your energy will show itself to be a gentle flow of power (a close aura—softer colors, just more condensed). So, is any one type of aura or power preferable to the other? No, not really.

Every Witch's energy signature or aura is different and unique, as is every person. There will be times when the most outgoing, high-voltage person is quiet. Their energy doesn't run full blast all of the time. If this person is working magick for healing, they would be more careful and subdued. If you are shy, for instance, and you work magick to make yourself stronger and more outspoken, then you would deliberately raise your energy and your aura as high as you could to bring about the changes that you wanted. (Think of it as a lightbulb that you can adjust the brightness on.) There will be times when you'll want to turn the light up on bright, and times when the softer light will do. So, how do you raise that personal energy? You raise it with concentrated focus and a positive objective in mind.

Focus and Intent

Natural magick is all about focus and your intent. Magick seeks to create loving, positive change. This is accomplished by your emotions and by magickal acts of compassion and kindness. This change is generated with your personal energies and with the energies of the natural world around you. In magick, we purposely raise and then release this personal energy so that it can zip off to create the changes that we need. You can achieve a strong ability to focus by visualizing and by practicing. Here is a magickal exercise for you. We are going to practice raising, and then releasing, your personal power.

Step Number One:
Raising and Releasing Personal Power

Stand up, with your feet a little ways apart. You should stand in a position that feels comfortable to you, but do not close the energy off by crossing your arms or legs. Leave your arms at rest by your sides. Now, imagine your personal power—or picture your aura, if you prefer—growing bright around you. Close your eyes, if it will help. Imagine a little glimmer of bright golden energy running along your skin, only an inch or two high at first. When you can picture this shimmer of light, move on.

Okay, now I want you to make that energy expand and grow larger. Imagine that it surges and grows out into a full, shining halo of bright light around your whole body. (As you imagine this, you may feel a tingle, your face may grow warm, or you can even experience a rush. Don't be surprised if you find yourself holding your hands up, or your arms out to your sides.) Hold that expanded energy in place for a moment.

Visualize what you want to do with this energy. Let's say you want to be confident at that after-school job interview tomorrow. Then picture yourself calmly and confidently handling the interview and being offered the desired job. Hold that image in your mind for a moment.

Now, I want you to deliberately release the halo of light. Push it out with a smile, gently and firmly away from you. Imagine that the halo of light is swirling away from you. Your personal energy now spins happily out on a breeze and off into the world to go and do its assigned job. Thank the element of air for its assistance. A simple "Thank you, element of air" will do nicely.

Take a deep breath, and hold it for a second or two. Now slowly release your breath and crouch down and place your hands on the ground or the floor. Imagine you are drawing a calming, stabilizing, and strengthening energy from the Earth. (This calming technique is called "grounding and centering.") Stay there for a moment or two. When you feel that you are finished, stand up, brush off your hands, and congratulate yourself at raising and then releasing positive magickal energy for the first time.

The raising and releasing of energy is a pivotal part of spellwork and magick. All magick requires a strong, positive intention and a concentrated focus on the desired outcome. When you combine that focus with the natural rhythms of nature and the ability to direct your personal power toward a specific goal, you will create magick.

Step Number Two:
Positive Intentions

Remember, positive intentions are an absolute must when you work natural magick. There is no place here for anger, jealousy, or hatred. If there is one absolute rule that Witches live by, it would be this one: "Harm none." Witches believe in causing no deliberate harm to others, and in karma. Basically, karma is the philosophy that what you do and how you do it will influence your life and people's lives around you.

Bottom line, kids, karma is cause and effect. As in, what we send out with a spell, we will get right back. If you are kind to someone, then a kindness shall be repaid to you in turn. Therefore, it makes absolutely no sense to try and harm someone or to manipulate them with magick, because it will turn around and bite you right back. With magick, karma is very real—and a *lot* more in your face.

I don't care what you saw on TV or in the movies, or whatever nonsense your friend whispered to you about the horrors of "evil spells" while you were in the library and they saw you looking for books on magick . . .

Once again, Witches believe in a God and a Goddess. Real Witches do not work evil or associate with it. They instead work to help and to heal. The truth is often less tantalizing than fiction, but the truth is that Witches are good, loving, and moral people. If the mind is the most powerful tool in magick, then your heart—if not as equally important—would have to be a close second. Magick is love. And if you think about it, to be loved is a magickal thing.

Now that I've gotten you to thinking, let's move on to the subject of day-to-day magickal life. You may be wondering what is expected of you if you become a Witch. Wait, I want to answer that one right now. You are expected to be the best person that you can possibly be.

So, how does a "real" Witch live their life, anyway? I bet you'll be surprised by my answer. Are Witches really different from ordinary people? Can I spot one just by looking at them? The answer is both yes and no.

Are Witches Really Weird, Or Do They Just Dress That Way?

Contrary to popular belief, there is no Witch dress code. Witches come in all genders, ages, races, shapes, and sizes. But normally, you cannot spot a real Witch in a crowd unless they want you to. The nice middle-aged lady wearing blue jeans and working in her herb gardens is much more likely to be a Witch than the guy you saw at the mall with the dyed black hair, multiple piercings, black fingernails, and all-black clothes. Witches and other magick users strive to blend in and work in harmony with the world around them, not to draw attention to themselves. Real Witches are normal people, just like you and (gasp!) your parents.

Ye Gods, no! you might think to yourself. *Witches can't be normal, can they?* We are. Witches come from all walks of life and social backgrounds. We are blue-collar workers and office workers. We have jobs at the grocery store and at the mall. Witches can be moms and dads. We are in the stands cheering our kids on as they play sports or as they participate in school plays or band concerts, just like all the other parents.

Witches are students, teachers, editors, waiters, factory workers, shop owners, dog groomers, electricians, and insurance salesmen. We can be lawyers, mechanics, paramedics, police officers, artists, bartenders, writers, horticulturists, nurses, and doctors. The list could go on and on. I have personally met or known Witches from all of the jobs described above. You never know, you may have already met several Witches and have not even been aware of it.

The reality is that Witches go to work or school, raise our children and love our families. We work to protect the environment and to keep our neighborhoods safe. Witches deal with all of the same problems that everyday or mundane people deal with: crabby bosses, bills, car repairs, nosy neighbors, school shopping, and hauling our sick children to the doctor.

The difference is we will help and protect ourselves and our families with magick, if we feel the need arise. We ask the God and the Goddess to assist us as we work to improve our lives and the lives of our loved ones with happiness, health, and prosperity in a positive, life-affirming way.

The Road to Discovery

Well, I've given you an overview of Witchcraft and natural magick. We talked about the tradition of Witchcraft and some of its principles and beliefs. You have tried your hand at a healing ritual, and then you practiced meditating and the raising and releasing of personal power.

You are just beginning this journey, and you have much more to learn. Are you ready to look at the natural world around you with new eyes? There are some amazing things out there waiting for you to discover them.

Remember, as you work your way through the rest of these chapters, your mind and your heart are absolutely the most potent tools that you have available to you. If you believe in yourself and are willing to work for it, just about anything is possible for you.

Ethics: Rule of Three

A Teen Witch Rule of Three

If you use magick to force your way,

A painful price you may have to pay.

If you do harm, you'll eventually get zapped!

Three times three is the ultimate payback.

For magick, good or ill, shall return to its sender,

This Witch's rule you must always remember.

The opening charm is one that I wrote for my teens. It is a tidy little poem to keep in the back of your mind as we discuss ethics, the Witches' law of nonmanipulation, and the Rule of Three. I debated whether to put this chapter further in the back of this book, but I am a firm believer in telling it like it is. Before you go any further, it's time for some straight talk. You need to understand exactly what you are getting into. Witchcraft is not all about cute spells that rhyme or dressing in funky black clothes, you know. Witchcraft is a lot of work. Witchcraft and natural magick follow strict rules and a code of ethical behavior.

Ethics may be defined as (*a*) a theory or system of moral values, and (*b*) the discipline dealing with what is good or bad, and with moral duty or obligation.

Laws? Ethics? Rule of three? "Oh, come on," some will say, "we just wanted the spells!" Now is when the dabblers (and by "dabblers" I mean people who play around with magick because they are bored or want to get even with someone) start to sigh and roll their eyes.

"You mean I don't get to turn my annoying little brother into a toad? Aww, come on, Ellen," they'll complain, "how about the most popular girl in school? You know, she's rich, beautiful, and mean as a snake? She is just awful to me! I can't put a hex on her either?"

Nope. If this is what you are looking for, than I am happy to say you are about to be hugely disappointed. This chapter will separate the teen occult dabblers from the real Teen Witches.

Dabbling: Don't Go There

If you have the guts to study Witchcraft, then you better have the guts to learn and follow its rules. Pay attention, now, here is an amazing magickal secret that I am about to share with you. Are you ready? Do you think you're strong enough to handle it? Okay, then . . .

True magick is about discipline and ethics. Effective spellcasting hinges on one emotion, and that emotion is *love*—knowing the difference between right and wrong and harming none. And I do mean none. Not other people, their possessions, plants, animals, or even yourself. *N-O-N-E* none.

The Wiccan Rede (*rede* is an old word for "law") states the following: "An' it harm none, do what you will." The Rede is both simple and complex at the same time. Basically, the Wiccan Rede tells us that we can do what we'd like with magick, as long as we don't hurt anybody else.

However, before you get all excited and think that world domination is about to be yours, think again. Notice that "harm none" comes before the "do what you will" part. Do you think there might be a reason for that? Of course there is. Witches and other magick users follow a nonmanipulation rule as well. This nonmanipulation rule basically guards against doing magick on another person without their permission, as in love spells.

It is unethical to perform a love spell on another because it involves messing around with another's free will. Would you want someone to take away your freedom and your right to choose whom you fall in love with and when? No way. To exploit another person or their emotions with magick is one of the worse things that you can do. I promise you that eventually you'll get zapped back in a bigger way than you can possibly imagine. That's the magickal rule of three. What you send out, good or bad, you will get back—times three.

If you're wondering why I am jumping into the topic of love spells right away, well, let's face it. Teens who dabble are usually in it for revenge of some kind. The "I'll get even with you for dumping me" type of thing. Or "You hurt my feelings by gossiping" . . . whatever.

Teens who are interested in practicing the natural art of Witchcraft will buckle down, study, and learn. So here we go, Teen Witch. Get ready for your first spellcasting lesson.

LESSON NUMBER ONE:
Love Spells Are More Trouble Than They're Worth

Love spells that target a specific person are a really bad idea. Now, you may magick yourself to seem more appealing or attractive. That is perfectly acceptable. Spells that call for you to have more confidence and poise are great too. You could try carrying a rose quartz crystal in your pocket to promote self-love. Picture yourself being surrounded by a rosy-pink glow. Be kind and polite to others. Smile! You'd be amazed at how well that works. If you are a happy, confident person, others will be drawn to you. If, however, you sulk, brood, or are overly sarcastic, people will avoid you. That old saying of my mother's is still very true: "You catch more flies with honey than you do with vinegar."

Finally, you may draw a happy, fun, and loving relationship into your life. Simply ask for the correct person (not a specific someone) to be drawn to you of their own free will. This may bring you a new friend and possibly a new boyfriend or girlfriend. It has also been known, in some instances, to bring a loving pet, such as a cat or a dog, to your home. But never, ever work a love spell on a specific individual or try to draw a particular person to you through magick.

The trouble with dabblers is that they'll try anything once, just to see if it really works. Let's think about this for a minute. What if it actually worked? And the point here is that it can. A dabbler will read a spell that says it's for binding a loved one to you and they get all hot and bothered, anticipating an adoring, devoted love slave for a boyfriend or a girlfriend. Get real.

Do you really want someone in your face, hanging on you obsessively, all the time? That would grow old, awfully fast. And, lest we forget, there is that Rule of Three to be considered. I'm going to give you an example of a love spell that turned out to be horribly more than a young dabbler counted on. The sad thing is that this story I'm about to tell you is true. And I had warned the dabbler of the dangers of manipulative spells many times. She simply refused to listen.

A young, college-aged woman came to me for a tarot reading at a psychic fair where I was working many years ago. She was lovely, blonde, and soft-spoken. As she sat down at my table, I noticed an unfortunately large, red scar across her forehead. *Car accident* flashed into my mind as she shook my hand. The scar looked very painful and recent. As the girl sat down, she looked like she was about to burst into tears.

She shakily informed me that she was here to find out what direction her life was now taking. The reading showed me the Tower card, in the past, meaning accidents and a shocking event. The card that represented her present situation was the Moon. This card portrays disillusionment. Her future card was the Queen of Swords. This card sometimes means a strong-willed woman who stands alone, or one who is looking for revenge.

The young lady's next card symbolized the best course of action. It was the Four of Swords. This card is traditionally explained as a time for rest and setting personal boundaries. Her "other people" card showed the Ten of Swords, which literally translates to other people betraying her and being stabbed in the back. Her obstacle card was the Hanged Man, a transitional card showing a happy fellow hanging upside down from his foot, from a tree branch. This card is traditionally interpreted as a life in transition. Her outcome card was very positive, however. It was the Star. The Star stands for hope, peace, and healing.

How accurate was I? Very, it seems. In fact, this young woman had been in a car accident, hence the scar. Her fiancé couldn't handle the fact that she had been scarred and broke off the engagement close to the wedding day, leaving her shaken, disillusioned, and depressed.

I gave her a pep talk and assured her that better days were to come. I agreed with her that she was better off without the moronic ex-fiancé, and now she needed to focus on getting her strength back. She should work on healing for herself and her broken heart. I helped her pick out a few stones to keep in her pocket to reinforce her healing: a rose quartz—the ultimate stone for warm fuzzies—a bloodstone for physical healing, and an amethyst for peace.

A few months later I saw her again. Her scar was fading and now she wore her hair in bangs. You could hardly notice the scar anymore. She seemed confident, happier, and guess what? She had discovered magick. Proudly, she displayed her new book. I was cautiously optimistic for her, and I recommended a beginner-level book and suggested that she study and learn her basics.

"Oh, no," she told me, "I'm having too much fun with spellcasting to study." She then started to ask me about love spells and bindings. Now I was getting nervous; what was she up to?

I told her very plainly about the rule of harming none and unethical castings. She just stared at me, plainly confused. "Didn't you read the book?" I demanded.

"What for?" she asked. So, big deal, she had skimmed it. She only wanted the spells anyway. She brushed my warnings aside and chattered on about getting even with her ex-fiancé. She had found a spell that would "bind him to her for all time." It must be working, she announced. They were starting to see each other again. She told me that she planned to make him sorry that he had ever dumped her.

I tried again, more forcefully this time. I grabbed her by the hand and told her to stop. I hauled her over to my table and gave her a very strong lecture on ethics and nonmanipulation. As a matter of fact, my voice was raised. A few people turned to stare as I tried to get it through her thick skull that what she was doing was not only wrong, but that it would surely backfire. It just wasn't worth the cost, I insisted. She only laughed and told me not to worry so much. She then waltzed away, with not a care in the world.

Several months passed and I did not hear from her. Then late one night I received a phone call. She wanted to ask me a question. In a very small and frightened voice, she explained to me that she had contracted a sexually transmitted disease, very recently, from the ex-fiancé. (The permanent kind, not the stuff that goes away with a dose of penicillin.)

It seems that he wouldn't leave her alone anymore. He thought that now, since they both had the same disease, they should stay together, forever. She wanted to know if all of the spells that she had been performing on him had anything to do with her contracting the disease and his obsessive behavior.

Very quietly I asked her if she had indeed "bound him to her" with a spell. She replied that she had. In fact, she admitted that she had done so, over and over again.

I was amazed. "Even after I warned you what the consequences would be and told you not to?" I asked.

"Yes," was her reply. She was sobbing now.

"Do you recall me explaining to you the rule of three? And how what goes around, comes around?" I asked her.

No response, she was too busy crying.

I sighed. "Well, honey, I hope you're happy. Because it worked. You wanted to be bound to him for all time . . . looks like you got your wish."

She hung up and I never heard from her again.

When I tell you that love spells and bindings on a specific person are never a good idea, remember this story and please believe me.

LESSON NUMBER TWO:
Working Magick for Another?
Get Permission

The rule of nonmanipulation also covers doing magick for another person. Manipulation occurs when you control or play on another person or their emotions in a sneaky or unfair way, for your own advantage or to get what you want. You want an example? How many times have you seen a spoiled toddler throw a tantrum in the store checkout line to get the candy that they demand? That spoiled child knows if they throw a big enough tantrum, their parents will give in. As soon as the child receives the treat, the crying and screaming shuts off like a light switch. The child wins and the clueless parents have no idea why the child acts up every time they go to the store—a perfect illustration of manipulation.

Back to magick. If you are wanting to magickally help another, you must have their permission. This is to avoid the karma and psychic backlash that may come from attempting to control or manipulate another with magick. The other person must either verbally request it or put it in writing. That way, there are no repercussions on you. Occasionally you may receive a request or two from someone who knows you very well. It will be up to you to decide if the request warrants a spell or not. We already went over the "Sally asking for a love spell to make Tommy fall in love with her" scenario—a definite no.

A harmless request once came to me from a relative who asked me if I would "do my thing" and help them with the sale of their house. They had an inspection coming up and she was worried that there would be a problem. I made my relative ask me specifically to work magick for her. She laughed nervously and then made her request. I did the work and it all went well. They passed the inspection and sold the house quickly, in about two weeks. Request made, spell performed, results obtained, everybody was happy. Simple and safe.

If you do decide to work magick for another person, getting permission is your safest bet, even if your intentions are good, like in a healing. Otherwise, you are still manipulating them with magick. What do I mean by this exactly? I'll explain it to you with an imaginary situation.

We will suppose that you want to help your grandmother. Let's say she fell and broke her hip and she is now going to have hip replacement surgery. Because you adore her so and you know that she has a long way ahead of her with therapy and such, you decide to work magick for her. *Perfect!* you announce, and then rub your little witchy hands together and start to plot.

"Let's see," you say to yourself, "I'll set out a few turquoise tumbling stones for healing, I need to go check the almanac for the perfect day and moon phase . . . Hey, the moon is almost full. That's cool, now all I need is a blue candle . . ."

Hold on a minute, my little Witch friend. Did you remember to get permission? If you did not, your choices are very limited and here they are.

- You may pray for her—and yes, Witches do pray.

- You may send your grandmother loving energy, that her guardians can then help her turn subconsciously into healing energy. In meditation, you should contact her guardian angels. Ask that if the loving energy you send out is acceptable to them, that she may then receive it.

- Or you can flat-out ask your grandmother. Try something like this: "Grandma, would you mind if I lit a candle and prayed for you to get better faster?" If she agrees, than do just that. If she refuses, then simply pray for her.

Remember, you should add a rider at the end of the prayer or spell, something like, "For the good of all, with harm to none." The reason for this little rider on the spell? Because sometimes things still can turn out weird, or not in a way that you had hoped for.

Why, you may wonder? If you didn't intend any harm, and were only trying to help, what could possibly be so bad about that? Because you are still manipulating the person. Noble intentions aside, you are still manipulating for what you want. This, unfortunately, may not necessarily be correct for the person you are targeting.

Once, when I was a much younger, less-experienced Witch, I sent my grandmother a physical boost of healing energy by way of a big hug. I had spent the holidays with her and she was, to my alarm, much frailer than I remembered. So, when I went to give her a hug and a kiss goodbye, I purposely gave her a mental boost of "I love you, be strong, you are invincible!" type of energy. Afterward I was a little drained, but I was worried about her and at the time I rationalized it by thinking that the energy boost couldn't hurt her, it would just make her feel stronger. After all, was I a Witch or not? A little extra shot of energy couldn't hurt anything. Could it?

Actually, it could. A week later, my grandmother, who was a tough, stubborn old bird, decided to forgo her usual walker and was cruising around her apartment. She got a little too cocky and overdid it. She fell and broke her arm. My mother fussed over her and then remarked to me about how my grandmother thought she was invincible. *Oops.*

Now do you get it? Think about it before you start casting. Mull over all the possible outcomes. Be absolutely sure. If you're not, let it sit for a day or two and come back to the decision when you're calmer and more levelheaded. That is a good plan many Witches would be advised to follow, and one that I follow myself.

LESSON NUMBER THREE:
Defend? Yes. Attack? No.

Defending yourself is perfectly acceptable. Attacking another with magick is not. Don't go looking for trouble or bragging about your magick to others, or you may find yourself in some pretty uncomfortable situations. If you're in a tight spot, though, you may turn negativity or hatred back to its sender. Some folks will talk about sending loving vibrations to a hateful person. I don't buy into that. Why give them more of your energy? Use that energy instead for protection.

Here is a handy little trick. You may protect yourself with an energy shield. Imagine the anger bouncing off of you because of a bright blue ring of fire or a blue armor that surrounds you.

Oh, and guys . . . be smart. If you even think that you might be in any sort of physical danger, remove yourself from the situation immediately.

Blue Shield of Fire
Visualization

To practice raising your own blue energy shield, close your eyes, and take a deep breath. Let it out slowly. Now, picture in your mind a neon-blue ring of protection that's been conjured by your own personal power and imagination. You could adapt our "raising personal power" exercise from chapter 1, if you need to. (Instead of imagining a yellow light shimmering around you, turn the color to a neon blue.)

Think "Shields up!" and, when you get to the "expand the energy out" part, toss that halo of light down onto the ground, where it blows out into a fiery ring of protection that will completely surround you. Hold this imagery in place for a moment or two, as you get away from the person or problem. If you hold this ring of fire visualization too long, it will probably make you tired and crabby afterward. This visualization and the following magickal spell are meant to be used for a few moments, not for an hour or two. Some variations on that theme of "blue fire" are as follows.

Some folks may like to visualize the classic Witches' big blue sphere of protection. Think of a large bubble of bright blue light that envelops you, both over your head and under your feet. This visualization can be enhanced by adding the phrase,

As above, so below.

All around me protection grows.

I personally like to imagine a big, bubbling sapphire cauldron at my feet. I came up with the idea of a sapphire cauldron because the sapphire is a magickal and protective stone. The contents of this deeply blue and gleaming cauldron bubble, boil, and then spill over the sides. As the liquid hits the ground, it forms a mist of glittering, blue-colored protection all around me. While using this visualization, I have had negative people abruptly back away and then complain about how warm they suddenly are feeling.

Some teens may want to picture themselves in a medieval type of armor in glowing blue. Go with what works for you. Visualize the angry person's hatred bouncing off your armor, mist, ring of fire, or bubble of protection and harmlessly melting away.

Try this protective spell to go along with your visualization:

While I'm safe here within my bright shield of blue,

All anger and negativity now returns to you.

Leave me alone and go bug somebody else,

Your temper will soon make you ashamed of yourself.

Safe from all harm, I forever shall be

And as I will it, so shall it be.

Work for harmony and acceptance before defending yourself becomes an issue. If things in your life are starting to turn sour, start working to fix things right away. Don't wait until you're in so deep that you have no idea where to begin. We all have days when it seems like everybody is out to get us, those horrific times when everything seems to go wrong all at once. The family is squabbling, the teachers are grumpy, your friends are moody, and your boss is quite possibly schizophrenic. Your car needs a new muffler and now, to top it off, you've just really ticked off your boyfriend or girlfriend and you haven't a clue as to why.

Sounds like you have your work cut out for you. Don't worry. When your life hands you lemons, try this modern interpretation of an old, reliable Witch's spell for breaking negativity and bad luck.

Lovely Lemon Ring Spell

For this spell, you will need:

- an ink pen

- a piece of yellow paper

- a lemon

- a knife (to cut the lemon into slices)

- a small plate

- a cup of salt (sea salt or table salt will do)

This spell will take about an hour of your time. Take the pen and paper and make a list of all of the problems in your life, and the possible, practical solutions. Take a good look at your list. See how many of those solutions you can achieve today. For example: crabby teacher? Did you turn in all your assignments? Solution: Finish the assignment and see if you can do any extra-credit work to bring your grade up.

Family squabbles? I bet they stem from somebody who's not pitching in. Solution: Run the vacuum without being told to, or clean your room. You can't work magick in a sloppy environment anyway. (It makes for sloppy magick.) I'm not kidding. You need to remember that magick works the best when you use it in conjunction with common sense.

Set your "to do" list aside, just don't forget about it. Now, cut the pointy ends off of the lemon. (Please be careful with the knife.) Dispose of the ends. Then slice the lemon into five equal slices. Arrange the slices on a small plate in a circle, in a rough star shape.

As you sprinkle the lemon slices with the salt, completely cover them up (use plenty of salt) and repeat the following charm:

In this lovely ring of lemon rounds,

no more anger will be found.

Sour feelings go to sour fruit,

pay attention now, I'm giving you the boot.

Salt breaks up bad luck and negativity,

my love and energy sets this spell free.

By all the power of three times three,

as I will it, so must it be.

Repeat the verse twice more; you will have said the charm a total of three times. On the last verse, take your index finger and draw a counterclockwise spiral in the air over the plate. Draw the spiral faster and faster, higher and higher until you fling the energy off your hand and out into the world. Brush your hands off three times and announce:

The spell is sealed.

Take that list and tuck it into your backpack or notebook. Try and accomplish as many of the solutions on your list as possible, either today or tomorrow. Put your things away. Set the plate in a spot where it won't be disturbed. Watch the lemons carefully; you'll want them to dry out and shrivel up. (It will take about a week.) Sprinkle them with more salt if necessary. If the lemons start to mold, dump the lemons and start the spell all over again. When you go to dispose of the shriveled-up lemons, dump them in the garbage, wash the plate, and put it away. If you've accomplished your "to do" list, toss that in with the lemons as well.

In natural magick, it is common to employ items such as herbs or flowers and sometimes even fruit. In this case, the lemon used in this Lovely Lemon Ring Spell is a symbol for the element of water. The salt, on the other hand, is a representation of the element of earth. When you are done working through the rest of this book, come back and see if you can identify how the remaining two elements, air and fire, are at work within this spell.

LESSON NUMBER FOUR:
Never Perform Magick When You Are Sick or Angry

Remember how we discussed personal power? Well, if you are sick, your personal power gets a little screwy. You'll have a hard time staying focused when you are ill, and your energy is more difficult to control. That is not a good thing. Likewise, if you are angry, you cannot make rational decisions. Your emotions are too involved.

You get so busy thinking, "Why, I oughta . . ." instead of, "Whoa, hey, I shouldn't!" If I am ill, mad, or upset, I do not perform any magick. I won't go near my tools and I give myself at least a twenty-four-hour cooling-off period. Why? Because you get fewer nasty repercussions that way. I have had my hands smacked by the Goddess a time or two for stupid magickal mistakes, and I like to think that I have learned my lesson.

If I am still not sure of the best thing to do, I may meditate on the situation, or call a magickal friend for advice. If none of that works, I light a tealight candle, thus invoking the element of fire, and say a prayer to the Lord and Lady and request their guidance. Then I take a deep breath, leave the situation in their capable hands, and walk away from the problem.

Ask any Witch who's been at this a while. Everybody makes a mistake eventually. The trick is to learn from them. This last rule is told to you here simply to help keep you from making a foolish error. If you cannot be absolutely calm, reverent, and controlled, leave magick alone.

That is why experienced Witches remind newer Witches over and over about the rule of three and nonmanipulation, usually because we've been there, done that, *and* bought the T-shirt. When in doubt, simply pray. Pray to the Lord and the Lady for their help and for their guidance. Listen to them and to your own heart. You will know what to do.

The following magickal principles were written by the late Scott Cunningham. These rules are straightforward and simple. You would do well to remember these, always. (From *Llewellyn's 2002 Magical Almanac*, page 192.)

Cunningham's Magickal Principles

- Magick is natural.

- Harm none, not even yourself, through its use.

- Magick requires effort. You will receive what you put into it.

- Magick is not usually instantaneous. Spells require time to be effective.

- Magick should not be performed for pay.

- Magick should not be used in jest (as a joke) or to inflate your ego.

- Magick can be worked for your own gain, but only if it harms none.

- Magick is a divine act.

- Magick can be used for defense but should never be used for attack.

- Magick is knowledge of its way and laws, and also of its effectiveness. Know that magick works!

- Magick is love. All magick should be performed out of love. The moment anger or hatred tinges your magick, you have crossed the border into a dangerous world, one that will ultimately consume you.

A Place for Your Thoughts

Here is a place for you to write down your thoughts about the rule of three and ethics.

What personality qualities do you imagine makes for a good and ethical Witch? Before you sigh and think to yourself that this is a total waste of your time, you may want to reconsider. Take a moment and jot down your thoughts on what you have learned about both Witchcraft and natural magick so far. This is your personal journal, so feel free to note your own opinions and ideas.

A PLACE FOR YOUR THOUGHTS

A PLACE FOR YOUR THOUGHTS

A PLACE FOR YOUR THOUGHTS

A PLACE FOR YOUR THOUGHTS

II
The Elements of Nature

Everything in **NATURE** contains all the
POWER of nature.
Everything is made of
ONE HIDDEN STUFF.
—RALPH WALDO EMERSON

THREE

The Element of Earth

Let's take it from the top. The four elements of the natural world are earth, air, fire, and water. These four elements are powerful tools and energies for the Witch to tap into. Each of them has their own unique magickal correspondences, with their own distinct magickal applications and specialties. In case you're wondering, a magickal correspondence is an index of things that complement or work in harmony with one another.

Each of the four magickal elements harmonizes to a different direction, a time of day, a season, a traditional magickal color, and an optional Witch's tool. For example, here is a quick list of correspondences for the element of earth. The coordinating direction is north and the season is winter. The traditional color for earth is green. Crystals, stones, and herbal magick all align themselves with the element of earth. The Witch's tool that represents the element of earth is the pentacle.

When working with natural magick, you are attempting to bring together natural items to help unify and tie your spellwork together. So, if you wanted an earthy representation for each of the four elements, you could experiment with these items: a feather for the element of air, a candle flame or lava rock to represent fire, a seashell to symbolize water, and a crystal or a live plant for the element of earth. Each of these suggested items is a natural embodiment of an individual magickal element. They each coordinate with their specific element, their magickal energies flow nicely, and they work in unity together.

This chapter and the next three are each dedicated wholly to a single magickal element: earth, air, fire, and water. A brief guided meditation is there for you to try. These meditations, or lessons if you prefer, will introduce you to and teach you about each of the four natural elements.

Following the meditation is a correspondence chart for that chapter's specific element. A correspondence chart is a quick reference guide for magicians and Witches. Plainly put, it helps you determine what works best with what. Then you will find a little information on the elemental being or nature spirit that is associated with that chapter's topic. There will be spells and charms that coordinate with each chapter, such as crystal and stone magick for the earth section, and so on.

If all of the information in the correspondence charts doesn't sound familiar to you yet, hang in there. I want to give you this information for a reference and for you to build on. So, before you get in a twist about the tools and doodads: we'll cover those later. They are *optional* and not absolutely necessary to perform natural magick.

Earth Meditation

What do you think of when you think of the element of earth? Close your eyes and let your imagination wander. Are you getting some good mental images? Do you see fertile green fields and massive old trees turning brilliant colors in the fall? Perhaps you imagine a garden. Pick out a favorite image of the earth. Now, find yourself a comfy spot and settle in. If you like, you may use this story as a pathworking or a guided meditation. Or, if you prefer, think of it as more of an illustrated lesson.

Imagine a forest filled with old, towering trees set against the backdrop of ancient, sturdy mountain ranges. Now, picture yourself walking safely through this forest. In this primeval forest, the deer, wolves, and bears roam free and undisturbed. You can almost smell the pine trees as a breeze rustles the various leaves overhead. Ferns grow tall, thick, and lush around the bases of the trees and perhaps a small, clear stream tumbles by. Small wildflowers dot the edges of the stream. You bend down for a closer look. Didn't your grandmother call those funny looking white ones Dutchman's breeches? You stroke a fingertip along a flower and watch them dancing in the breeze.

As you walk alongside the stream, you find an interesting creek pebble. It is rough in shape and has a hole through it that is slightly off-center. Thinking that it's a pretty souvenir, you stuff it into the pocket of your blue jeans. You stand still for a moment and take in your surroundings. It is so easy to imagine yourself in another time and place here. The forest is cool, calm, and reverently quiet. The only sounds that you hear are the trill of birdsong and the occasional chatter of a squirrel. You decide to try your hand at meditating and scout out a likely spot to stretch out for a while. There, under the big oak tree and along the stream, you find a mossy spot and settle in.

As you tuck yourself alongside the rocky stream, you are relaxed and at peace. There, surrounded by a sense of permanence, stability, and strength, you watch the patterns of the sunlight as it dances through the tree branches. You begin to feel better, lighter, as all of your troubles start to drain away. It almost feels like the earth is sending you healing energy as you sit on the ground, beneath the trees. Completely relaxed, you lie back and begin to doze off.

A short time later, you are awoken by a rude poke in the shoulder. You sit straight up to be confronted by a small, gnarled old man. He is dressed in rugged greenish-brown clothing and a red vest. He has a long, gray beard and a balding head. The old man can't be even three feet tall. Weird. You shake your head and wonder if you are still dreaming. For good measure, he pokes at you with his walking stick again.

"Dreaming? Ha!" He frowns at you. "Look real enough, don't I?" He stands there, leaning on his tall, polished walking stick, and stares you down. He is trying to look intimidating, you imagine, but the mischievous sparkle in his eye is giving him away.

As you rub your shoulder and are about to complain about the rude way that you were woken up, you catch yourself and you smile. Magick is definitely afoot.

"Hello," you say carefully. "Pleased to meet you."

"Hmpf," he sits down easily next to you. "At least you have manners." From somewhere in your mind you realize that this is a gnome—an earth spirit. Your heart starts to speed up in excitement. How cool is this? He stares out at you from under wiry and thick beetle brows and demands to know why you have fallen asleep in his forest.

"Your forest?" you ask.

"My forest," the gnome repeats and puffs up his slight chest. "I am Ghob, the caretaker of this place." With a sweep of his arm, his gesture takes in all of the land that you can see. From out in the distance, the roar of a bear and the howl of wolves echoes through the forest. A cool northern breeze dramatically sends the branches to swaying until, with a sweeping motion of his walking stick, it all becomes quiet again.

Impressed and at a loss for words, you watch him and wait to see what he will do next. Your mind races a hundred miles an hour as you try to think of something intelligent to ask him. Finally, with a lack of anything else to say, you blurt out, "I really like your forest."

The gnome grunts and nods his head in agreement.

Well, you decide, *that was certainly brilliant*. As you wonder what to say or do next, a doe and a stag quietly approach the stream across from you. You hold your breath and become completely still as they come closer. They nimbly step their way to the stream and take a drink. You start to grin at how close they have come and how utterly unafraid they are. You risk turning your head slightly to see what the gnome is doing. He is smiling at you. The gnome speaks softly to the doe and she bobs her head as if in answer. After a few moments, the pair bound off right past you and into the forest. You turn your head to watch them until they disappear into the greenery.

"What do you seek?" he asks quietly after a moment.

"I'd like to learn more about the element of earth," you manage.

He nods his head in agreement. "This is the magickal sign of the element of earth," he tells you as he scratches a symbol in the dirt with his walking stick. It looks like a circle with an equal-armed cross through its center.

"In magick, the element of earth stands for strength, stability, prosperity, grounding, and the Earth Mother Goddess," the gnome explains to you.

"What's grounding?" you manage to ask. "I've heard of that before."

"That's what you were doing under this tree a short while ago," he informs you. "When you found a nice quiet spot and imagined all of your troubles and burdens draining away into the ground—like sinking roots into the soil, as a tree does. That would be grounding."

You silently nod your head at him in the affirmative, and he continues.

"Now, the animals that are associated with the earth element are the wolf, the stag, and the bear." He looks at you intently to make sure that you are paying attention. "Each of these animals has a gift and a lesson to teach you. From the wolf comes the courage to find your own path in life, and the gift of cunning." He stops for a dramatic moment as a chorus of wolfsong fills the air. You shiver and he smiles blandly.

"From the deer you acquire agility and swiftness," he continues.

"Okay, that makes sense," you comment as you recall the pair of deer at the stream.

"Strength and love of family are the offerings of the bear. Do you understand?" he asks.

You answer yes, that you understand. Then you think to yourself that you sincerely hope you will not be meeting a bear anytime soon.

The gnome smiles mischievously, as if he knows where your thoughts lie. He rises quickly to his feet and leans his walking stick against the tree trunk. Now he reaches into his vest pocket. "Here," he hands you a palm-sized smooth stone. "This is for you. Keep this with you. This will help you to remember that the element of earth is to be found in the stones, the trees, and the plants of the forest. Use this stone to get in touch with the element of earth. Keep it with you, in your pocket if you like. Then you can rub the stone when you start to worry too much. It will help ease the tension."

"Sort of like a worry stone?" you ask him.

"There are many ways to learn from the stones. But you can call it that if you wish," he tells you.

"What about this one?" you ask him as you pull the creek stone out of your pocket.

The gnome's eyes light up. "Ah . . . a holey stone. These are very special indeed." He takes the stone from you for a moment as he looks it over. "Found yourself a treasure, didn't you?" The gnome hands the stone back. Then he tells you with a gruff smile to take good care of his children.

"I will," you say, smiling at him. As you admire first your rough holey stone and then the smooth flat stone from the gnome, an idea pops into your mind. You wonder if it would be all right to paint the magickal symbol that he showed you on the smooth stone.

"Of course," he pats you on the head as he replies to your unasked question. The gnome does know your thoughts after all, you realize with a jolt.

"Paint the symbol green," he demands as he starts to walk away through the underbrush and into the forest. He stops and turns to look over his shoulder at you. Then he chuckles, "It's my favorite color."

You smile back and start to put the stones into your pocket. "Wait!" you call after him, as you jump up to follow. You have so many other questions. . . . You lunge to your feet, prepared to run after him. But he is nowhere to be seen.

Suddenly you wake with a start. Did you imagine it? You get up slowly and begin to look around you. You pat down your pockets, checking for the stones. You reach in and pull out a rough creek stone and a palm-sized smooth rock. Your heart starts to thump in your chest, as you make your way back to the tree. You take a few steps, then you stop cold. There in the dirt, right next to where you had been sleeping, is a symbol scratched into the ground. You crouch down to take a look at it. It's a circle with an equal-armed cross in the middle. It's the magickal symbol for the element of earth.

Shakily, you reach out to lean against the tree for a minute and catch your breath. As you reach up to steady yourself, a tall, polished stick falls against you. You recognize this. It belonged to the gnome from your dream. You sit down onto the ground with a thump. *Was it a dream or was it real,* you wonder as you admire the staff. Did he leave it for you, then? It would make a great walking stick, it's about the right height for you. You decide to ask out loud if you may keep the walking stick.

A breeze rustles through the trees and you hear his voice softly say in answer, "It is a gift. You will need it for your other journeys. Be aware that I will send to you more elemental beings. Give them your respect and consider carefully the lessons that they will teach you."

You rise to your feet and thank the gnome for his gift, wherever he may be. As you stand for a moment to look around for any sign of the gnome, you decide to tie the holey stone to the staff to decorate it.

"Good idea," his voice comes from somewhere behind you.

You turn to look behind you, but all you can see is the greenery of the forest.

"I'll use a green cord. I know it's your favorite," you answer with a chuckle. Then, with your new walking stick in hand and stone treasures in your pocket, you begin the journey home.

EARTH CORRESPONDENCE CHART

Direction: North

Color: Green

Time of Day: Midnight

Season of the Year: Winter

Places: Gardens, mountains, forests, and woods

Witch's Tool: Pentacle

Deities: Artemis/Diana, Earth Mother, Flora, Green Man, the Great Mother Goddess, and Pan

Symbol: ⊕

Animals: Bear, wolf, and deer

Elemental Being: Gnome

Magicks Include: Prosperity, grounding

Natural Representations Include:

- Salt and soil

- Crystals and stones

- Herbs, trees, and plants

The Earth Mother Goddess

The Earth Mother is believed by some to be the embodiment of all nature spirit activity and garden energy. Cultivated within the wisdom of the Great Goddess, the Earth Mother presides over all trees, shrubs, plants, and herbs. It is thought that the Earth Mother is actually an embodiment of all of the angels, elemental beings, nature spirits, and faeries combined. If you want to get to know the faeries and the nature spirits, you are going to have to work with and gain the respect of the Earth Mother.

The Earth Mother transforms the love and energy of these magickal creatures into the physical forms of nature and beings by incorporating all of the four elements. The four elements, as well as all of nature, are governed by the guardianship of the Earth Mother.

When I close my eyes and imagine her, she has ebony, flowing hair and a soft, rounded face with a dusky complexion. Her green eyes are wise and her smile is full. My Earth Mother's flowing robes are green, gold, and deep brown. Her gowns are rich and fragrant with the scents of herbs and the soil. Surrounding her are the many varieties of nature spirits. Some hover close by her for protection, while other winged sprites merrily zip around her head.

To me, the Earth Mother embodies home, comfort, magick, and fruitfulness. Close your eyes and focus your imagination on the idea of an Earth Mother. How does she appear to you? There is no right or wrong answer. Every person's perception is unique. Everyone will see what they need to see.

Remember when I first told you that to be a "real" Witch required an open and loving heart? Well, you are about to put that into practice. To call on the Earth Mother, you must be pure of mind and heart. In other words, leave the day-to-day stresses and negativity behind you. Try contacting the Earth Mother during meditation at sunrise or during a time of day that you can be calm, peaceful, and relaxed.

Pick your time and be properly prepared. Take a bath, wear clean clothes. Lose the watch and leave the phone inside. Settle quietly down in the backyard, the garden, or any other safe and comfortable spot in nature for a little one-on-one with the Earth Mother and the earth spirits. Close your eyes and request that they make themselves known to you. Relax and let your mind drift. See what images come to you. Listen to what messages they may have to teach you. Bring along a notebook and leave your preconceptions behind. Write down what you see and feel.

If you have a natural affinity with the Earth Mother and earth elementals, you may end up having a visit from a nature spirit during your meditation. The nature spirit may be male or female. They can be tree spirits or earth devas. You may be very surprised at what she or he has to teach you. When you are finished with your meditation, thank the Earth Mother in your own words, and then thank the nature spirits for their company and time.

Close your meditation and visit with the elementals by using this verse.

A Thanks to the Nature Spirits Charm

To the elementals and nature spirits who have gathered near,

I release you with my love, I thank you for your presence here.

Return safely now to your home, from whence you came.

By the powers of the green earth and the silver rain.

By saying this, you ensure that the nature spirits return safely to their natural habitats. Basically, if you are going to call in the nature spirits, be polite enough to let them know that you appreciated their time and help. This verse is a polite way to let them know that you are finished, thank you very much, and now you're sending them back home.

A Little Information on the Earth Elementals

Each of the four elements has its own nature spirit to go along with it. These nature spirits or elemental beings often share the characteristics of the element that they are assigned to. For example, one of the four types of elemental beings are the gnomes. They are earthy and hard-working. The gnomes are the earth elementals and the guardians of the treasures of the earth. Gnomes are the protectors of the sacred places in nature, such as the woods and forests. They help to make the trees and the plants grow, and they preside over crystals and gemstones. The gnomes guard the earth and all of her mineral treasures. Historically, gnomes have often been grouped together with other earthy spirits, such as the faeries and the elves.

Before you start imagining these elementals as cute little garden gnomes with pointy red hats, let me point out here that these are *earth* spirits. They are made up of the energy of the earth. They can vary in their appearance and you won't normally find them peeking out at you from around a tree stump in the forest. Gnomes and other earth elementals, such as elves, tree spirits, and land devas, usually work with us by way of lending their energy to our spellwork.

If you politely ask for their assistance, they are usually happy to lend you a hand, so to speak. Since gnomes are earth spirits, you could call on them for help in any "earthy" type of natural magick that you perform. Garden magick, working with plants and flowers, and crystal magick is, of course, their specialty. The gnomes and other earth elementals would also complement spells for stability, prosperity, creativity, and craftsmanship.

Crystals and Stone Magick

Crystals and stones are used for quite an assortment of magickal purposes. Stones and crystals are prizes from the earth and the earth spirits that we can use to enhance our magick and our lives. Stone and crystal magick is a relatively straightforward concept. When you work with a stone or crystal, you are bringing its powers and energies into the spell.

How you direct those powers to your desired goal is what makes the magick.

By using your powers of visualization and imagination, you can literally program the stones (that is, you tell them exactly what it is that you want them to do). For example, let's say you have a monster history test coming up. You've already studied your little brains out, but the thought of taking that test still makes you a nervous wreck.

So, you would take an amethyst for peace and an agate for bravery and hold them in your hands, and ask the God and Goddess to help you to be confident and calm when exam time comes. Focus your intent and your will on the stones. Raise up your personal power and tell the stones that you are asking them to lend their energies to you for a time. Tell them what you are asking for. Be specific. Say something like this:

Help me to be confident and to do my best

when I take this history test.

Then slip those programmed stones in your pocket, like a talisman, and off you go.

If you need to reinforce the magick come exam time, take the stones out of your pocket and hold them in the palm of your hand. Recall what it was that you programmed them to do. Now, ground yourself. Imagine that you are sinking roots deep into the soil, as a tree would. Imagine that the earth is sending you stability and strength. Take a deep breath, then blow it out. Pocket the stones and go ace that test. It is just that simple.

Having some tumbling stones on hand is an easy way to learn to work with crystals and their various energies. You can usually find a good variety of inexpensive tumbling stones at a nature shop or a metaphysical store. Experiment with the various stones and their energies. Try keeping a few in your pocket and see how you react to them. Do you notice any difference? Do any of them make you feel queasy? Amber does that to me. I don't know why, it just does. I have a friend who always feels lightheaded when she carries a malachite stone. Different crystals will influence different people in various ways.

Try putting a few complimentary crystals around a candle and see how well that works for you. For instance, looking for a good after-school job? Put in several applications at places you'd like to work—places that you feel you would be a good employee. Then try burning a green candle for prosperity and place an aventurine and a tiger's-eye on either side of the candle to help draw success and money. It is up to you to decide if you want to add a little spoken charm to go along with this magickal experiment. Maybe you would prefer to let the natural energies already within the stones silently do their work. Ultimately, it is your decision and either way will work just fine.

Here is a quick reference list of the magickal properties for some easy-to-find crystals and semiprecious stones. See how well you and your magick work with crystals. Investigate these for yourself and keep notes!

CRYSTALS AND SEMIPRECIOUS STONES

Agate: Agates come in many colors. Its general magickal uses are strength and bravery.

Amethyst: For peace, happiness, and power. A good all-around stone.

Aventurine: For good luck and prosperity.

Bloodstone: For health, healing, and reducing stress.

Carnelian: Encourages love and good health.

Hematite: A God stone. Inspires grounding, stability, and healing.

Malachite: Will bring fast cash, business success, healing, and protection. If your malachite stone should suddenly break, it is a warning of coming danger.

Moonstone: A Goddess stone. Moon magick, safe travel, and intuition.

Obsidian: Deflects negativity and is a protective stone. It also makes a good worry stone. (Remember the lesson from the gnome?)

Quartz Crystal: Add a quartz crystal to any other stone to enhance the stone's power. Quartz crystal by itself is a tool for protection and directing energy.

Rose Quartz: The ultimate warm, fuzzy stone. Love, friendship, and happiness.

Tiger's-Eye: Protection and success.

Turquoise: Protection, friendship, and good fortune.

Spells and Stones

Here are some short, sweet, and simple spells for you to experiment with.

Protection and Balance Spell

This stone spell comes in handy for the times when you feel that a little extra protection is called for—when things in your life seem a little off-balance, out of kilter, or perhaps unfair. This stone spell will enforce a little extra protection and it will work to put things back into alignment, to basically even the scales.

Supplies needed:

- One moonstone and one obsidian stone (small tumbling stones will do quite nicely). If you cannot locate tumbling stones, substitute a white rock and a black one.

- One white and one black votive candle. (I like to use small votive candles, as they are inexpensive and easy to find.) Votive candles will burn for approximately six to eight hours.

- Two glass votive candleholders.

- A safe, flat surface to place them on.

- A lighter or matches.

Try working this spell at sunset. Since we are working for balance, performing this spell at an in-between time (when it is neither night nor day) is ideal. Place the candles in their holders. Arrange the stones and the candles in this order: moonstone, then the black candle, white candle, and the obsidian (so when these items are all lined up, it will be: white rock, black candle, white candle, black rock). Light the candles and repeat this charm three times.

> *White light of day and black of midnight,*
> *help me to set all problems to right.*
> *All is balanced, as night and day,*
> *keep all harm and injury away.*

Close the spell by adding,

> *For the good of all, with harm to none.*
> *By the moon and stars, this spell is done.*

Leave the candles to burn until they are completely gone. Keep an eye on them. For safety's sake, never leave a burning candle unattended. If you have to leave the candles, move the candles and the stones to someplace safe, like the bottom of the bathtub, inside the fireplace, or in the kitchen sink to finish burning.

If for some reason you cannot do this, don't panic. Snuff the candles and relight them at the following sunset, repeating the spell as you relight them. When the candles have burned themselves out, keep the stones together and on your person. Tuck them into your pocket or backpack for as long as you feel that you need them.

Prosperity Spell

Is money tight at home? Are you really strapped for cash? Try this spell to help ease the crunch. Be prepared to earn the money by working for it. I see babysitting jobs and lawn work in your future.

Supplies needed:

- One plain tealight; it will burn for approximately four hours.

- A glass jar to burn the candle inside of. Old glass canning jars are perfect for this.

- These four tumbling stones: turquoise, tiger's-eye, aventurine, and malachite.

- A lighter or matches.

- A safe, flat surface to set up on.

- A small quartz crystal point—this will be a gift to the gnomes for their help.

Perform this spell anytime of day or night. Set this spell up so that you face the direction of north, the direction associated with the earth spirits and the element of earth. Try to perform this spell outside, if possible. If you are worried about a breeze blowing your candle out, place the tealight inside of a glass jar. Place the jar with the candle in the middle of your working surface, and set the four stones around the outside of the candle jar in a loose circle. (Set the small crystal point aside—you will be leaving that in the garden for the gnomes when you are finished.)

Once again, never leave a burning candle unattended, especially outdoors. Try setting up on your back porch or patio—maybe you could use the top of your picnic table?—anywhere you are well away from flammable items, like dry leaves and such. Light the candle and repeat the following charm three times:

> *Little golden and green stones and candle burning bright,*
>
> *gnomes, I ask you for the chance to earn money tonight.*
>
> *Tiger's-eye, turquoise, aventurine, and malachite,*
>
> *All will aid in this spell, turning out just right.*

Close the spell:

> *By all the powers of three times three,*
>
> *as I will it, so shall it be.*

Place the small crystal point that you had set aside in the yard or the garden. If you live in the city or an apartment and do not have a yard, then tuck the crystal point into a flowerpot or leave it someplace in the park—try under a tree or a shrub, or perhaps in a flower bed. Then, after leaving the stone, quietly announce that it is a gift for the gnomes in thanks for their friendship and help.

Leave the small quartz point for the gnomes, do not try and take the gift back. This is rude and will offend the earth spirits. Let them keep it. Allow the spell candle to burn out. Pocket the four tumbling stones that were around your candle and keep them with you for a week. See what money-making opportunities present themselves.

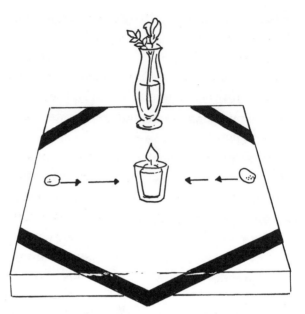

Drawing Friendship Spell

This spell may be used to draw a new friendship to you. We are not targeting a specific person here, just asking for a new friend to find their way to you of their own free will. As you recall, we went over the particulars of manipulative magick in chapter 2. If you need a refresher, flip back to the second chapter and reread lesson number one and lesson number two. Please note: This spell will take a few days to complete.

Supplies needed:

- Two rose quartz crystals.

- A pink votive candle. Pink is a color often used for friendship spells.

- A glass votive candleholder.

- One pink rosebud or a zinnia from the garden, in any color. Why flowers? Well, flower magick is one of my specialties. You'll find more information on flowers and their uses in natural magick in chapter 7. In magick, a pink rose may be used for friendship and a zinnia signifies faraway friends.

- A bud vase or small glass to hold the flower.

- A lighter or matches.

This spell would be a good one to work at sunrise, as the sun lights up the sky from a rosy pink to bright blue. This way, you could incorporate the energies of the new day and fresh beginnings into this spell that is asking for a new friendship.

Place the candle into the holder. Set the two rose quartz crystals on opposite sides of the candle, about twelve inches away from the sides. Place the flower into a bud vase and set it directly behind the votive holder, also about six to seven inches away. This will keep the flower safely away from the heat and flame of the burning candle.

Repeat this charm three times. At each repetition of the spell, scoot the two crystals closer to the candle. (The two rose quartz crystals symbolize you and your new friend, coming closer together and finding each other.) As you say the final repetition of the charm, the crystals will be resting next to either side of the candleholder.

> *Two rosy pink stones and a sky so blue,*
>
> *send to me a friend whose soul will be true.*
>
> *May we recognize each other, and become great friends,*
>
> *by the powers of earth, fire, water, and the four winds.*

Close the spell by adding,

> *For the good of all, with harm to none.*
>
> *By flower and leaf, this spell is done.*

After the candle burns out, keep the stones with you. When you find your new friend, give one of the rose quartz crystals to them as a token of your new friendship.

As to your flower, leave it in the vase until it begins to fade. Then take the flower outside, crumble the petals in your hands, and scatter them upon the ground around you in a circle. (If you used a rose, be careful of the thorns on the stem!) You may dispose of the flower stem by throwing it away or adding it to the compost pile when you are finished. You may quietly announce, "This spell is sealed."

Note: This is the spell that I mentioned before. It has been known to sometimes draw a new loving pet into your life, instead of a person. Why? Well, trust the God and Goddess to know what is best for you. After all, friends may come in many wondrous varieties.

Want more information about working with stones and crystals in magick? Start cracking a few books open. Look around in the New Age section of the bookstore and see what you can find. Here are a couple of my favorite books on the topic of crystals. Think of these suggested books as tools to help you expand your understanding and studies on crystals, natural magick, and the element of earth.

Further Reading

Cunningham, Scott. *Cunningham's Encyclopedia of Crystal, Gem and Metal Magic* (Llewellyn, 1992).

Whitaker, Charlene. *Gems of Wisdom* (Cosmic Connection Publishers, 1987).

FOUR

The Element of Air

In this chapter we will learn about the magickal element of air. Use your imagination again and see what natural images come to mind when you concentrate on the element of air. Do you imagine a vast meadow dotted with wildflowers? Windswept prairies and plains, or high, rugged cliffs and canyons? All of these places are associated with the element of air.

Air Meditation

Imagine that you are embarking on a nature hike for the morning. You have packed your backpack with a lunch and a drink and off you go. You also have with you the walking stick that was a gift from the gnome Ghob. Your holey stone swings gently on a bright green cord that you attached to the staff a few days ago.

As you walk along the meadow path, you wonder if you ever will see that old gnome again. The morning is bright, warm, and breezy. Pleased with yourself and your morning, you tip your head up to watch as big puffy clouds billow past. As you stand there looking up, a strong, flowery scent drifts to you. What is that smell? It's so familiar. You close your eyes and turn your head, trying to pinpoint the source of that amazing fragrance. The meadow grasses sway and the flowers dance in the wind. Following your nose, you step off of the path and walk farther into the meadow.

The grasses are taller here, and the flowers more colorful. Occasionally birds shoot out of the grasses ahead of you, scolding and squawking at the interruption. You slow down, trying not to disturb any more wildlife, and make as little noise as possible. A pale yellow butterfly flutters overhead and you turn to watch it instead of watching where you are going. That's a mistake. You are so busy watching the butterfly that you step in a hole, turn your ankle, and fall down onto the soft ground with a thud.

You sit there for a moment, nursing your twisted ankle and muttering. Great. You peel down your sock and take a look at your ankle. Sore, but not swollen. You give your ankle an experimental twist to see how bad it hurts. Okay, it does hurt. You use your walking stick and pull yourself up to your feet. You take a step. Ouch! You look around to find a good place, hopefully in the shade, to give yourself and your ankle a rest. Alongside the meadow are a trio of trees. That's not too far to walk, you decide. And it's a likely spot to eat your lunch as well. You wade deeper into the meadow, toward the trees, grumbling the whole way.

You make it to the trees and prop your walking stick against a large, smooth trunk. You brush aside a few fallen acorns and gingerly lower yourself down onto the meadow grass. Deciding to make the best of the situation, you lean against the tree trunk. You root around in your pack for your lunch and the water bottle and take a swig. As you begin to eat your lunch, you start to relax, watching as dragonflies hum by and several butterflies chase each other in and out of the tall meadow grasses. A moment later, a yellow butterfly flutters over and lands on your water bottle.

"Scram," you tell it, as you shoo it away. "You're the one that probably got me into this mess."

The butterfly insistently comes back. You grin at the butterfly as it lands on your water bottle again and again. The scent of the flowers is much stronger here, deep in the meadow. A pair of blue jays lands in the branches overhead and loudly scolds you for intruding on their turf. You tear off a piece of crust from your bread and toss it onto the ground for them with apology.

As you finish your lunch, you begin to notice the sound of bells. Almost like wind chimes or jingle bells, they shiver and sigh in the breeze, loud for a moment and soft as a whisper the next. Intrigued, you look around. Did someone hang wind chimes from the branches of the trees? Tipping your head back, you study the branches. The one you're leaning against is an ash. The next one must be an oak. What's the other tree? It has some pretty impressive thorns on the branches. Could it be a hawthorn? That seems significant and you struggle to remember why.

Now the bells sound like they're right on top of you, coming from everywhere and nowhere all at once. That scent that first led you here is rushing in on a breeze, both strong and sweet. Your head spins and you close your eyes and put a hand to your head to stop the rushing feeling.

The music reaches a crescendo and then suddenly stops. You carefully open your eyes, to be confronted with a much different-looking meadow than you were sitting in only a moment before. The colors are deeper and truer and it is very quiet. You sit still and listen for a moment. No sounds of traffic or planes. Just birdsong and the faint music of the faeries singing.

Faeries singing? That thought stops you short. You start to get up, totally ignoring your ankle, to look around you. The flowers in the meadow seem bigger and brighter. And you realize, as your heart bumps up to your throat, that the petals are moving. It's not from the breeze either. There is something tending to them and it's way too big to be a bumblebee—could it be a hummingbird?

Carefully you edge closer to a bright yellow wildflower. You reach out a hesitant hand and then stop in amazement at the little winged sprite busily hovering over the petals. You snatch your hand back and stare in wonder at a rather industrious little faerie. "They *are* real," you breath in astonishment.

"Well, of course we are real," it answers you back smartly. The faerie zips in a circle around your head, and then stops about three inches from your nose. You quickly try and gather impressions. Is it male or female? Female, you decide as it fluffs its golden-blonde hair and preens. With tiny hands on tiny hips, she grins at you. "Don't be so surprised," she teases you. "After all, didn't you come here looking for a bit of magick?"

"I'd like to sit down," you announce as you stagger over to the tree trunk and plop down. It follows you and zips around the tree in a few quick circles. You're getting dizzy just trying to follow its track of flight. In defense, you shut your eyes for a moment, only to feel something settle on your knee. Cautiously, you open one eye to discover the faerie has perched on your knee and is regarding you with a puzzled expression.

"You are not what I was expecting," the faerie announces.

"I'm not?" you ask.

"No. Aren't you going to try and catch me?" She frowns petulantly at you as she smooths down the saffron-colored skirt of her dress.

"Well, no," you explain. "I've done a little reading on the elemental kingdom."

"Have you, now?" The faerie brightens up at that.

"I read that you are supposed to be very careful around the faeries and only show them respect." You pause and it motions for you to continue. "You guys like to play tricks on people."

You wait to see how she reacts.

"Oh, aye. That we do," the faerie admits with a giggle. "But you've been most polite and, to reward your good manners, I will grant you a boon."

"What's a boon?" you ask suspiciously.

"A favor, a gift," the faerie explains to you patiently, as if you are a little slow.

You consider carefully. "I'd like you to teach me about the magickal element of air."

The faerie grins at you. "Then teach you I shall." She settles in and gets comfortable on your knee. "In magick, the element of air is used to bring about change," the faerie informs you as a fragrant breeze flows by. "It may be used to boost your creativity and for studying and seeking knowledge."

The faerie pauses for a moment as a trio of dragonflies zooms by. With a smile, she continues. "The creatures associated with the element of air include winged animals such as the birds and, of course, flying insects. Particularly the bee, the ladybug, and the dragonfly."

"What about butterflies?" you ask, thinking of the yellow one that you noticed earlier.

"Well, of course," the faerie chuckles at you. "That's how we got you here, after all."

You narrow your eyes at the faerie. "That's sneaky."

"No. It's tricky. I've a fondness for a good prank." The faerie flutters up and settles over on the ground next to you. At a signal from the faerie, a pair of blue jays lands close to your feet and they squawk for a moment to her. Amazed, you watch them carry on some type of conversation. Then, seeming to reach an agreement of some sort, the blue jays fly away.

The faerie holds up three fallen feathers triumphantly. "Tough negotiators, those blue jays. But here you go," she states as she rises up to your level.

Carefully, you accept the feathers from the faerie. "Thanks," you tell her.

"Now pay attention," she informs you as she hovers in front of your face. "The gifts from the birds are many, and each bird carries a unique gift. The feathers of the blue jays may be used to bring about creativity and adaptability. You may pick up fallen feathers, but never take any from a live animal. For no feather that crosses your path is left there by accident. Do you understand?"

You nod your head and answer yes. Suddenly a group of butterflies flutters around the trees where you are sitting. Enchanted, you turn your head to watch as they sail around you. They flutter happily about until the trio of dragonflies whizzes past and disrupts them.

"Now, the gifts of the butterflies are joy and transformation," the faerie informs you. "The gifts of the dragonfly are change and illusion. You may combine these two magicks together if you choose, for a glamoury." Then, in a lightning change of mood, she warns you. "Have a care, though, how you use these magicks."

"Isn't that where you use magick to change your appearance?" you ask.

"In a way. A glamoury is a technique that changes other peoples' perceptions of you, not the actual color of your hair or eyes."

"Isn't that pretty devious?" you ask.

"Of course. The Fae are experts at glamouries," she announces proudly.

"Which would be why I should be careful." You think on that for a moment. How easy would it be for a glamoury to backfire? Sounds sort of like manipulation, you decide, and that would not be a good thing.

The faerie has landed on your knee again. "I have to go soon," she announces. "But before I leave you, I want to show you something." She points to the ground where a symbol has been drawn with yellow flower petals. The symbol is a triangle with one point up, and it has a horizontal line drawn through the center. "This is one of the magickal symbols for the element of air," she informs you.

"Wouldn't these be a symbol as well?" you ask, as you hold up the feathers.

"Oh, very good!" she applauds.

You study the symbol on the ground and think on it for a moment. Yellow butterflies and now yellow flowers? "Is yellow a color for the element of air?"

In answer, she rises up and pats the side of your cheek. "Aren't you clever!" she says proudly. You share a smile with your diminutive teacher.

You begin to notice the sound of bells and chimes again. You tip your head up to look. "Are there wind chimes around here?" you ask her.

"Yes and no," she tells you as she flies back toward the meadow.

You rise to your feet and follow her. "There is or there isn't?" you ask.

The faerie gently laughs at you. "You tell me." She darts over to a wild purple aster and begins to work over it, as the sounds of bells and laughter ring in your ears.

You start to feel lightheaded and that rushing feeling is coming back to you. You close your eyes again, waiting for the swirling feeling to subside. The bells become impossibly loud and then—silence.

You open your eyes to find yourself still seated under the ash tree. You look up as you hear an airplane fly overhead. Obviously back to the world that you left behind, you feel slightly bewildered. But now that you've seen what you have, will you ever look at things the same way again? Still in your hand are the three feathers. You smile at them and recall that she didn't even give you the chance to say thank you.

How long was she with you? You notice, without surprise, as you check your watch that hardly any time has passed since you started your nature walk.

"Well," you say to yourself, "she said they were fond of tricks." You gather up your lunch, careful not to leave any trash behind, and get to your feet cautiously. The ankle seems fine, so you shoulder your backpack and gather up your walking stick. Those feathers would look nice if you tied them onto the staff with another cord . . . a yellow cord, you decide. You stop and tuck the feathers into your backpack for safekeeping.

You turn to look at the place where you just spent the last hour or so, and realize with a start that the three trees are meaningful. An oak, ash, and thorn is the faerie trinity of trees. You consider them for a moment and decide to leave a gift for the faerie who helped you. You dig around in your pocket for the tumbling stones that you were carrying. You choose an amethyst and set it carefully at the trunk of the ash tree, quietly whispering your thanks. Then, finding the meadow path that led you here, you turn down it and begin the journey home.

AIR CORRESPONDENCE CHART

Direction: East

Color: Yellow

Time of Day: Sunrise

Season of the Year: Spring

Places: High places, such as mountaintops, meadows, and windy plains

Witch's Tool: Wand

Deities: Aradia, Aphrodite, Arianrhod, Butterfly Woman (Native American), Eros, Mercury, Nut, Psyche, the Sky Father

Symbol: △

Animals: Birds and flying insects—bees, butterflies, dragonflies, and ladybugs

Elemental Beings: Faeries, sylphs, and flower faeries

Magicks Include: Creativity, knowledge, study, and change

Natural Representations Include:

- Feathers

- Flowers

- Oils, perfumes, and the perfumed smoke of incense

A Little Information
on the Air Elementals

The elemental beings most often associated with the element of air are the faeries and the sylphs. Sylphs are described as nature spirits that use the element of air; they are identified with clouds and storms. The sylphs are the spirits of the four winds, and the mystical, moving force behind the energy associated with air and magick. What do they look like? Well, imagine a kind of ethereal air spirit—a translucent-looking type of angel or "fairy." However, sylphs are not cream puffs. Sylphs are beautifully wild and strong. You may hear their voices in the howling storm winds as they call back and forth to each other. Sylphs are a rather potent type of energy, a natural force. If you call on or invoke the sylphs, you will bring excitement, increased knowledge, and change into your life.

I have a little advice for you here. If you are grown up enough to study magick, then be aware that in petitioning elemental beings such as the sylphs or faeries, you may cause repercussions that you were not expecting. No whining if things suddenly change drastically! If you petition the sylphs for change without being specific, they will bring it. In other words, be very particular and be careful what you wish for.

Faeries are also associated with the element of air, as are scented flowers. It is believed that each plant and flower has its own spirit or faerie to guard over it and to help it grow. This is probably how the idea of flower faeries most likely began.

Flower faeries may appear to us in a variety of ways. I have never seen a winged Tinkerbell type of faerie myself. However, I have seen the flowers and plants quiver and bounce for no apparent reason as I worked in my gardens. I have had tree limbs shake and shiver in a yes or no response when I requested a leaf or a small twig for a spell. I heard a quiet, bell-like music that I could not explain one Beltane night. Members of my family have seen unexplained balls of colored lights in the woods while they were deer hunting.

You never know how the faeries may appear to you. Most likely you will catch movement out of the corner of your eye, or you may feel them walk through your hair. You know that feeling, it gives you goose bumps. Then, as you quickly pat your hair down, there isn't really anything in your hair at all.

In my book *Garden Witchery* I told readers about the time, when I was a very young Witch, I called in house faeries, just for the fun of it and because I was curious about what would happen. That old saying really applies here: "If you call them, they will come."

We were overrun with a type of earthy house spirit called brownies. Those we saw. They were small, brown, and moved incredibly fast. The kids loved it, but the brownies caused tons of mischief and trouble until I finally asked them to move out into the garden instead.

Incense: A Little Goes a Long Way

The scented smoke of incense represents the element of air and can help to set an excellent magickal mood. I have found that fragrant incense helps you get in touch with the air elementals a little easier. Incense is used in magick to purify an area or an object. The incense smoke may be lightly fanned over an item or a person to perform a smudging. A smudging is a psychic cleansing of sorts. The scented smoke clears away stress, negativity, and impurities.

Here is a Witch tip: Use incense sparingly. A single joss stick burning in the room is a pleasant experience, as long as you are not standing on top of it. However, if you get too much incense smoking away at one time, it might make you cough or sneeze. Set the stick or cone to the side. Allow it to burn somewhere in the room, just away from the immediate area where you perform magick. You want to enjoy the scent, not breathe it in.

If you want to burn the incense for only a moment or two, then use sticks. These can be tamped out quickly and left in the holder to light again at a later time. Tamp out the sticks completely in a fireproof metal lid or pottery bowl. Let them sit undisturbed for a time afterwards to make sure they are completely extinguished. Also, for safety's sake, don't leave burning incense unattended.

Some families have rules against burning incense in the home. I personally love a nice, light incense, but my kids can't stand it. I often threaten them with fumigating their rooms with incense if they don't clean it up to my satisfaction. It does an outstanding job at clearing the "locker room" smell out of my boys' room. I guess they figure if they leave piles of dirty laundry in the corners or under the bed, I won't see them. Here is an astounding but true fact for you to chew on: Mothers everywhere have a sixth sense about dirty laundry and messy bedrooms. It's a gift, don't question it.

If you are not allowed to burn incense in your room, you can still perform a cleansing by calling on the element of air. Here are some suggestions for you to try. Open a window and let the breeze in, or perhaps turn on a fan. Ask the sylphs, the air elementals, to cleanse the room of all negativity. If you feel the need for a psychic cleansing yourself, take a stroll outside and wait for a good breeze to catch you. Turn into the wind and face it. Hold out your arms and breathe in that wind. Ask for the element of air and the sylphs to cleanse you of all negativity. Remember, whether you are inside or outside, to thank the sylphs for their help when you are done.

The Magick of Music

Do you play a musical instrument? Are you in the band or orchestra at school? Do you sing in the choir? Lucky you, won't you have fun with this next magickal assignment! Sound and music, especially a voice or notes played from a woodwind instrument, are very complementary to the sylphs, faeries, and the air element. Try sitting out in your backyard some morning at sunrise and softly playing or singing a little tune to the air elementals. You don't have to be fabulously talented to do so, just enjoy yourself. It doesn't matter whether you play the flute, the trombone, the viola, or the electric guitar. Perhaps you like to sing. Go with whatever works for you. Use your passion for music to communicate with the air elementals. Try this little elemental charm to go along with your song and see what happens. If all you can manage is humming or whistling, then knock yourself out. Just get out there and connect with nature.

Air Elemental Musical Charm

Air elementals, this music magick I send to thee,
circle around, bring positive change for all to see.
As the winds of change now blow in,
grant me knowledge and wisdom.
Assist me in making my dreams come true,
the music I now play is a gift from me to you.

Wind Chime Magick

Still afraid to make your own music? Try hanging up some wind chimes. Look around for a set of wind chimes that sounds good to you and has a pleasing tone. Or look for a wind chime that has faeries on it, or any of these themes: butterflies, moons, stars, or suns. All are very witchy and enchanting. Enchant these chimes to bring about good fortune and protection every time the wind catches them. Try this little spell to bless them as you hang the wind chimes outside.

Magickal wind chimes, now be for me

a charm for good luck and prosperity.

As the chimes ring out, a spell they'll weave,

all dread and negativity now must leave!

By the powers of the sylphs and the faeries,

as I do will it, so now shall it be.

Bees, Butterflies, and Ladybugs

As a gardener, I love flying insects like the butterfly and the bee because they are pollinators. Many types of flying insects help to pollinate our flowers and our fruit and vegetable crops. Butterflies and bees in the yard and garden are a wonderful thing. They are the sign of a healthy and happy garden. In all the years that I have been gardening and working in nurseries and garden centers, I have never been stung by a bee. Why, you may wonder? Well, we understand each other. I respect them and give them plenty of room to do their job. I don't swat at them or bother them while they are busy gathering pollen.

I have had visitors to my gardens become somewhat alarmed when I am headfirst in the flowers and surrounded by several honeybees and bumblebees. They always look at me goggle-eyed when I calmly explain to them that the bees and I are busy simply doing our respective tasks. They pollinate the flowers and I care for the flowers. It's a team effort. Besides, if you leave the bees alone and don't panic, chances are they will return the favor to you.

Here is a perfect opportunity for you to get outside, commune with nature, and learn a magickal lesson all at the same time. Go sit someplace comfortable and settle in to study some flying insects and see what you discover. Now I do realize that some folks are severely allergic to bee stings. These individuals should take more care to avoid direct contact. If a bee is happily bouncing along among the flowers, then leave it alone. Find a blooming shrub or lovely flower bed and settle down and watch the insect activity from a safe distance, if this is a problem for you.

Winged insects are sacred to the element of air and the Faerie kingdom. The honeybee, for instance, has quite a tradition of old magickal folklore surrounding it. Bees were greatly valued in olden times as the makers of honey. A much sought-after food, honey was an important preservative. Honey was believed to be a source of wisdom and magick. This nectar of the Goddess was thought to be a cure-all, or ambrosia.

Bees are the sacred symbol of the Greek goddess Aphrodite. Priestesses of hers were called the *melissae*—in other words, "bees." The harvest mother/goddess Demeter was known as the "mother bee." Bees are regarded to be symbols of wisdom, prosperity, fertility, and the sun. These tiny, flying messengers are servants to the gods. The sound of happily buzzing bees was considered to be the voice of the Goddess herself.

If you have a beehive on your property, you are supposed to keep them informed of the family news, otherwise they will leave. If a bee enters your home, it is a sign of good luck. So don't kill the little bee! Try and shoo it out an open window or capture it and let it go outside where it belongs. If a honeybee lands on your hand, it predicts coming prosperity. If a honeybee settles on your head, it is a sign of coming fame. If a bee flies around a sleeping child, that child will be blessed with psychic gifts and enjoy a long and happy life. Bees are a sure sign to get busy and to get moving! Be a busy little bee, finish up those projects, and quit procrastinating.

The butterfly represents both transformation and the soul. *Psyche* is the Greek word for both "soul" and "butterfly." In Greek myths, the heroine Psyche was beloved by the winged god Eros. Their story is a bit like a "Beauty and the Beast"-type of tale. Through many trials and tribulations, they finally ended up together. In a famous painting by Adolphe William Bouguereau, Psyche and Eros are pictured happily together, and she is appropriately represented as having butterfly wings.

In some countries, the butterfly was thought to represent wisdom and the souls of children waiting to be born. In Irish myths, the maiden Etain transformed herself into a butterfly, then landed into the drinking cup of a queen and was swallowed, to then be reborn.

If a butterfly lands on you or you notice butterflies fluttering around you, this is a message from the God and Goddess to prepare yourself for a change. Perhaps it is time to transform old habits into something more positive. Pay attention to what color the butterfly is, as this will give you a clue of what you need to change. For example, if it is a blue and black butterfly, like a swallowtail, perhaps you need to lose some negativity or stress that you are carrying around and begin the process of healing. In color magick, black is used to absorb negativity and blue is a healing color.

Finally, here is a little folklore and magickal information about everybody's favorite garden bug, the ladybug. The red and black colors of the ladybug stand for health and protection. From a practical point of view, a garden full of ladybugs can mean one of two things. Either you have been blessed by the faeries, or you have pests called aphids. If it is the latter, then the faeries have sent in the troops to help you out. Ladybugs love to chomp on aphids. How to tell if you have aphids? Check your roses and the blooming shrub spirea. If there are ladybugs swarming on these plants, chances are you have an aphid infestation. The ladybugs are probably enjoying a feast of nasty aphids, so leave them to it. The ladybugs should neatly clear up the problem for you.

In England, our spotted friends are called ladybirds. Ladybugs/ladybirds are thought to be pets of the faeries, especially the ones with seven black spots on their backs. If a ladybug settles on your skin or hair, it is a sign of good luck. If you find a ladybug in the garden, you may scoop it up gently and let it crawl around on your hand. Make a wish and call upon the element of air for assistance. When the ladybug flies away on a breeze, it will take your request straight to the faeries.

Feather Magick

Feather magick is worked much the same way that crystal magick is. Birds are obviously associated with the element of air, and so too are their fallen feathers. As you begin to work feather magick, you will be working with the magickal associations of the birds that the feathers actually came from. A lone feather waiting for you in the middle of the sidewalk is no mere accident. It was left there on purpose. Pick it up to see if you can identify what bird it may have come from. Remember to look around with your new witchy eyes. What do you see? What do you sense? Pay attention to Mother Nature, she is trying to get your attention! Fallen feathers are gifts from the air elementals.

Every feather may, in fact, become a talisman. A talisman is an object that is believed to have magickal power and may act as a charm to both avert bad luck and to attract good fortune. A feather may be used as a magickal accessory. It can help you to interact and to form a closer bond with the magickal element of air and the natural world all around you.

For example, if you feel the need to defend yourself and your personal belongings, try adding a blackbird's feather to your spellwork. You could discreetly tie a feather or two onto a cord and carry it with you. If your belongings are threatened at school or work, you could try tucking one into your backpack, pocket, or even your locker.

If you happen upon a fallen feather, refer to this guide to see what lessons the air elementals are trying to teach you. Use this correspondence list for a quick reference guide to your feather magick. You may carry a coordinating feather with you for a specific need, or place a feather alongside a complementary candle or crystal in your spellwork.

Please remember that it is illegal to possess feathers from endangered or protected birds, like some species of the owl or the eagle. When in doubt, call your local conservation department.

BIRDS AND THEIR MAGICKAL CORRESPONDENCES

Blackbird: Defending your territory. "Back off."

Bluebird: Happiness and joy. "Be content with life."

Blue Jay: Creativity, adaptability, and speaking out. "Speak up for yourself."

Cardinal: Vitality and beauty. "You've brightened up my day."

Crow: Walk your talk. "Magick is to be found all around you. Don't be afraid to walk your own unique path."

Doves: Peace, love, and beauty. These birds are sacred to many goddesses. "Peace and joy to you."

Finch: Energy and home. "Sing your own magickal song." Goldfinches are rumored to live in places where there is a lot of faerie or nature spirit activity.

Goose: Travel. "Places to go . . . people to see!"

Hawk: Messages, power, and protection. The lesson of the hawk is, "Wake up and pay attention to the signs and messages that are around you!"

Loon: Dreams and imagination. "Follow your dreams."

Mockingbird: Pride in your accomplishments. "Anything you can do, I can do too!"

Owl: Magick and mystery. "Sit still, observe, and be silent; the answers are coming."

Peacock: Mystery, romance, and illusion. "Beauty is found within." *Note:* I do realize that the chances of stumbling across a peacock feather while you're out strolling around are slim. However, they are often found at craft stores and at various festivals. They are a large, fun, and gorgeous feather to own, and they are well worth having. These feathers will add a little drama to your feather magick.

Raven: Magick and shapeshifting. "Things are not always as they appear."

Robin: New beginnings. "Spring is in the air" and "Let's start fresh."

Turkey: Thankfulness and prosperity. "I am thankful for my life."

Woodpecker: Energy and activity. "Wake up! It's time to get going!"

As we close this chapter on the magickal element of air and winged creatures, don't forget to pay attention to the insects and birds that are in your life and living around your home. What messages do you suppose they have for you? Get out a notebook and jot down your ideas. If you would like to research this topic more thoroughly, check the reading list below. Open those eyes and really look at the natural world around you. There are many lessons to be learned from the creatures of the earth.

Further Reading

Andrews, Ted. *Animal Speak* (Llewellyn, 1994).

Andrews, Ted. *Enchantment of the Faerie Realm* (Llewellyn, 1993).

Nahmad, Claire. *Fairy Spells* (Souvenir Press, 1997).

Nahmad, Claire. *Garden Spells* (Running Press Books, 1994).

The Element of Fire

Of all of the elements, fire commands the most respect. It is beautiful, destructive, and creative, all at the same time. When working with this most volatile of the elements, caution and care are called for. In our attempts to learn more about this magickal element, we should be smart and safe with candles. I don't want you to accidentally set off the smoke detectors in your house. A good rule of thumb with fire and candle magick is to never leave burning candles unattended.

Besides a burning candle, the element of fire may be represented in other ways: the rays and warmth of the sun, the heat and intensity of summer, a lava rock, and the color red are all magickal correspondences for fire. Concentrate on the element of fire for a moment or two. What images do you conjure up?

The rosy-colored sun as it sets in the west? Cheerful fireplaces inside tidy homes? Dozens of flickering candles grouped together on a mantle that cast dancing shadows across the walls? Cozy campfires or powerful volcanoes and lava flows? It's time to take another journey in our elemental meditations. I think you'll like this lesson . . . it has a certain spark to it.

Fire Meditation

Imagine you are sitting in front of a cheerful campfire on a balmy summer evening. Dusk has just fallen and you plan to have yourself a marshmallow roast before too long. You give the fire an encouraging prod and watch the flames and the smoke shoot skyward. After a time, the smoke shifts direction and blows into your face. You wave your hand in front of you to dispense the smoke and shift your position on the ground. The logs hiss and pop as a large puff of smoke billows upward. Your eyes begin to water from the smoke, so you scoot back a little farther to avoid having any more blown into your face.

You enjoy watching the stained-glass colors of the flames and the coals—various shades of yellow, orange, and cherry red. You ease back and begin to imagine shapes in the flames. You blink as a shape begins to take form within the campfire. You sit up and watch intently as the shape becomes more defined. *What is that, a lizard?* you wonder. *No, it kind of looks like a little dragon.* Chuckling softly, you rub your eyes and look again. It's gone.

Amused at yourself and your imagination, you get out your marshmallows and stick and prepare to make yourself a snack. As you hold your marshmallow over the flames, they suddenly flare up. Annoyed, you yank your marshmallow back and give it a critical study. Almost burnt that one. You try a different spot, to find that the same thing happens. Whoops! It is on fire! Quickly you blow out the treat and, in disgust, toss it into the flames. You decide to try another one. After two more flaming attempts, you are totally baffled. *What's the deal?* you wonder.

"I like them burnt," a voice announces from somewhere in front of you.

You jump almost straight up in the air at the sound of the voice and grab for your walking stick. "Is someone there?" you ask.

No answer. The woods have fallen silent.

Your visibility is limited in the gathering darkness but you can still see around the immediate area. You spin around, looking to identify the owner of the voice. You hold your walking stick up like a quarter staff with the crazy idea of fending off an attacker. "Come out where I can see you," you challenge.

"If you insist," the deep voice says.

You hold your breath. Silence.

Cautiously, you watch for any suspicious movement. To be on the safe side, you decide to cast a protective circle for some extra protection. You walk around the campfire, scratching a large encompassing circle with the walking stick into the soft dirt. As you work, you imagine a bright blue flame running along the ground. You move back to the beginning of your drawn border and stop to center yourself. Then you raise up your personal energy and toss it down, where it spreads out along the edge of the indentation and reinforces the protective circle.

"By the powers of earth, air, fire, and water, I cast this circle. May this be a protected place and a sacred space that no one may enter." You walk around the inside of the circle once, twice, and then, finally, a third time.

"This circle is sealed," you say, and tap your walking stick onto the ground four times. Safe within your circle, you stand guard for a moment and wait.

No one is there. Feeling confident that you have frightened them off—and feeling rather proud off yourself for thinking to cast the protective circle—you sit back down, keeping your walking stick close at hand. After a few moments, the crickets start to sing again and you notice that the sounds of the woods have returned to normal.

Weirdo, you decide. Determined to enjoy your cookout, you spear another marshmallow.

As you reach toward the flames again with your treat, the entire campfire billows unexpectedly upward. With a little screech, you dive away from the suddenly ferocious flames. As your eyes water and sting, the air shimmers around you with heat waves. You watch wide-eyed as the impossibly tall flames begin to take shape. "Oh, crap!" you whisper. *What's happening? What is that?* Then your brain finally kicks in and recognition dawns. That thing taking shape within your once-little campfire is a dragon.

"Did you call me a weirdo?" it demands. The smoke and flames have formed into a rather large but more defined-looking creature. A huge black dragon with glistening scales and massive crimson and black wings is standing before you. The dragon's ruby-colored eyes narrow at you as your jaw drops.

Your heart slams into your throat and you rise to your feet, still clutching the walking stick. Now you've done it. You've just closed yourself inside of a cast circle with a fire elemental. A really pissed-off elemental, from the look of things. The heat is intense but you should be safe inside your circle. You hope.

The dragon shimmers incredibly with more heat and seethes bad attitude. "Well?" it rumbles.

Showing any fear would be foolish, you realize. You decide to take a stand and hope that you don't end up like one of your marshmallows. "Yes, I did call you a weirdo. You frightened me," you explain to the dragon.

As its answer, it seems to gather itself up, preparing to roar. The heat becomes blistering. You instinctively shield your face with your arms from the heat.

Immediately, the heat subsides. Cautiously, you lower your arms to regard the dragon. Clearly displeased at having to talk to a human, it looms over you.

"I was told," it announces in a voice that rumbles like thunder, "that you were on a quest." You are fairly certain that it is tapping a rather large, clawed foot impatiently at you.

"A quest?" you repeat. "I don't understand."

Incredibly, the dragon rears its head back and begins to swear at you. Wow. You had no idea that dragons had such an expansive vocabulary of curse words. Your fear begins to subside and you begin to enjoy the encounter. You are trying your best not to smile, but you can't help it. The dragon appeals to your sense of humor. Leave it to you to find the most trash-talking dragon on the continent. A half-laugh that you try to disguise as a cough escapes you. The dragon whips his massive head around to regard you with narrowed eyes. Immediately, you try to maintain a sober expression.

"Ghob, King of the Gnomes, told me to seek you out." The dragon simmers and seethes, but sucks in his temper.

"Ghob? He sent you to me?" you ask.

The dragon nods his head and narrows his eyes in displeasure for questioning him.

Quickly, you try to make amends. "I appreciate your time," you say sincerely. "You're more impressive than even I could have imagined," you tell him.

The dragon puffs up a bit at the flattery. "Naturally." The dragon accepts this praise as no more than his due. "I do not like to waste my time with foolish mortals, be they Witches or no. Casting the circle was clever, little one," it nods to you. "However, I was already inside when you cast it," he graciously points out.

"Oh, I see," you reply lamely.

The dragon leans its massive head close and sniffs you over. It nudges the walking stick and smoke blows out of its nostrils. Half terrified, half thrilled, you remain as still as you can.

With a nod, it announces, "You do carry the gift of the gnomes and I will fulfill my promise to Ghob."

"You mean my walking stick?" you ask him.

The dragon nudges you with his massive head, none too gently. You do your best not to get knocked off your feet. 'The staff, yes. But I smell other elemental beings around you," it decides.

"I had a visit with the faeries last week," you confide to him. Your hands itch to touch him, as he is right in your face, but you worry about upsetting him.

"Faeries, bah!" he says with disgust. "What could the little faeries possibly teach you?"

"She was very kind." You defend your faerie teacher.

The dragon seems to take no offense, but the grumbling and growling resume. "There are three gifts from the element of fire," the dragon suddenly proclaims. "Passion, enthusiasm, and courage."

You nod your head and remain silent. There is no sense in upsetting the big guy any further.

"The sacred animals of fire are the lion, the snake, and the lizard." With a lightning-fast move, he draws a three-sided symbol, surrounded by a circle, into the air. "This is the elemental symbol for fire." It glows red in the air and then fades.

"I thank you," you say formally. Since the situation seems to call for it, you bow your head.

The dragon growls impatiently. "I have fulfilled my promise. Release me from your circle."

"The circle is open, you are released." You say without hesitation. The fire and smoke collapses in on itself. Then, in a flash and a boom that echoes like thunder, the dragon is gone.

You stand for a moment, coughing and waving your hand at all the smoke. As your blinking and watering eyes clear, you inspect the remains of your campfire. It has completely burned itself out. Amazingly enough, there is no heat—only cold ashes remain. To be safe, you decide to keep an eye on the ashes for a few more minutes, and sit down and recall what lessons your cantankerous teacher had for you. *Passion, courage, and enthusiasm.* You consider these gifts carefully. All in all, you seem to be getting the hang of this "meet the elementals" routine. A grin spreads over your face as you recall the dragon's creative vocabulary and his regal personality.

You take your walking stick and carefully draw into the ashes the symbol that the dragon had shown you. It is then that you notice a burn mark running alongside your walking stick. The burn mark is in the rough shape of a dragon. You smile. Another elemental being has left its mark on the walking stick and, somehow, that seems just right. After a safe period of time has passed and you're sure that the fire will remain out, you pack up your belongings and head for home.

FIRE CORRESPONDENCE CHART

Direction: South

Color: Red

Time of Day: Noon

Season of the Year: Summer

Places: Fireplaces, campfires, volcanoes, and hot springs

Witch's Tools: A candle flame, the staff

Deities: Mars, Pele, Tiamat, Brigid, Apollo

Symbol: ⬭

Animals: Lions, cats, lizards, and snakes

Elemental Being: Dragon

Magicks Include: Protection, love, and healing

Natural Representations Include:

- Candle flames

- A campfire

- Lava rock

- Obsidian

- The rays of the sun

A Little Information
on the Fire Elementals

Dragons are the elemental spirits associated with the element of fire. For many cultures, dragons have been popular symbols of power and wisdom. Dragons represent vitality, energy, enthusiasm, and courage. In ancient Greece, Europe, and throughout Asia, the dragon was held in high esteem. In Europe, the dragon was often synonymous with the earth serpent. The earth serpents traditionally guarded buried treasures.

You may find it interesting to know that, in England, the symbol for Wales is the red dragon. This symbolism originated from the Great Red Serpent that once represented the old Welsh god Dewi. The red dragon was first placed on the royal arms of England by Henry VII, who was of Welsh descent.

The dragon was thought by the Chinese to be a spirit of "the Way," thus bringing eternal changes. White dragons, to the Chinese, represented the moon. Also, the dragon was the Imperial emblem of China. The Chinese dragons were commonly pictured with horns, claws, and scales, holding or guarding a pearl. Why a pearl, you may wonder? Because within the pearl lies the dragon's power. The pearl guarded by the dragon is the "pearl of wisdom."

If you are looking for a way to protect and defend your choice of spirituality and the knowledge that you have learned, try calling on the dragons for a little spiritual protection. Be polite when you call on the fire elementals. Don't waste their time with frivolous requests. Remember, they are bigger and much more powerful than you are. If you need protection or a boost to your courage, or some extra energy, the dragons will be more than happy to assist you.

Candle Magick

In magick, a burning candle represents, or is a symbol for, the element of fire. *Well . . . duh*, you're probably thinking. Hang on for a moment, guys, I want to explain. You see, fire is the spiritual principle of magickal transformation. Since all magick seeks to transform something, whether it is a situation or an outcome, that makes invoking the element of fire, or candle magick, a pretty powerful act.

Candle flames give off a mystic sort of power all on their own by changing the mood or atmosphere of the room in which they are burned. Imagine what wonders they can do in a Witch's knowledgeable hands. In magick, the burning candle is a physical symbol of your spell. As you focus your concentration on the candle, you load the candle with your intentions and with your personal power.

Candle magick may be combined with color magick and aromatherapy. Aromatherapy is the use of certain scents that may aid in the healing of the body and positively affect the mood. In aromatherapy, certain scents and fragrances are used to help boost your spirits or to alleviate headaches, fatigue, or stress.

As for color magick, it is used every day in subtle little ways that you may not even be aware of. Color influences our thoughts, our health, and our actions. Let me give you a few examples. Red roses for passion and love. A deep red dress that says, "Hey, look at me, I'm hot stuff." Don't forget the red "power ties" for men. Soft colors, like baby blue and pastel pink, are comforting and make you want to snuggle up. Here is another good one—hospital scrubs that the doctors and nurses wear are usually blue and green. Did you know that blue and green are both healing, soothing colors?

By using color magick in your spellwork, you may harness the magickal power of light and color. If you combine harmonious candle colors and scents together in your spellwork, you are adding more power to the magick. Think of it as a one-two punch. Well, look at you! Not only are you learning candle magick, you are also learning about magickal aromatherapy and the power of color. The following list is a correspondence chart on color and candle magick. Use this list as a springboard to get you thinking, and then to add your own ideas to later on.

COLORS AND CANDLE MAGICK:
MAGICKAL CANDLE COLOR CORRESPONDENCES

Baby Blue: Comfort, children, and harmony.

Black: Breaking hexes, banishing illness or negativity.

Blue: Peace, spirit, hope, calm, healing, and the element of water.

Brown: Grounding, happy homes, pets, and garden magick.

Gold: The God, riches, wealth, and fame.

Green: Prosperity, growth, healing, gardening, herbalism, and the element of earth.

Grey: Binding, banishing, invisibility spells, and glamouries.

Lilac: Clairvoyance, tarot work, and faerie magick.

Lime Green: Warding off jealousy, and springtime magick.

Orange: Energy, optimism, enthusiasm, action, harvest, and intensity.

Pink: Love, warm fuzzies, friendship, and children.

Purple: Psychic powers, personal power, self-worth, and magick.

Red: Love, vitality, healing, protection, summer, and the element of fire.

Silver: The Goddess, women's mysteries, the moon, and intuition.

Yellow: Creativity, communication, studying, spring, and the element of air.

White: All-purpose, peace, calm, and hope.

Common Cents Candle Magick

So many candle spells, so little time. . . . But, before you run out to purchase expensive beeswax tapers and large pillar candles, I want to give you a few practical Witch tips.

- A Witch is not judged by how much he or she spends on occult supplies.

- Votive candles are our friends (especially the fifty-nine-cent ones).

- Votive candles come in a wide variety of scents and colors, and are readily available.

- Votive candles burn for six to eight hours.

- To ensure easy removal of any leftover votive wax, put a teaspoon of water in the votive cup and then place the votive on top of it. As the votive candle burns and turns to liquid wax, the water creates an air pocket. When the candle is finished burning, you can easily pop out any remaining wax.

- Plain, white tealights are an inexpensive, all-purpose magickal candle. (They are available everywhere in packs of twelve, for usually under two dollars.) Twelve candles for two bucks equals approximately sixteen-and-a-half cents per candle! Now we are talking bargains!

- Tealight candles also turn to liquid quickly and burn for two to four hours.

- It is not necessary to anoint votive candles or tealight candles with essential oils.

I have read plenty of magickal books that insist it is necessary to anoint all of your spell candles with special essential oils. Rubbing a drop or two of oil onto a candle is a way to consecrate the candle and to bless it. Basically, by doing this, you are announcing that the candle is now a holy or sacred object. That is a fine thing to do, but the world will not stop revolving if you do not drip a little oil on your spell candle.

If you would like to anoint your unlit candles, go ahead. It is your choice and your decision. It certainly won't hurt anything. However, you should be careful and do your homework when working with the various oils. Sure, they smell wonderful and they are a great addition to a candle spell, but you should still be careful when handling essential oils.

Essential oils should not be ingested. Be cautious of skin allergies and wash your hands when you are finished using them. Avoid touching your face or your eyes when working with oils. (You don't want to accidentally get the oil into your eyes.) A final word of caution: Some oils may cause skin irritation, like pine or cinnamon. Cinnamon oil can actually burn the skin. Try using a dropper to put the oil on the candle, so you can avoid skin contact.

What if you do not have access to essential oils, or you're unsure about using oils—but you would like to try and anoint the unlit spell candle anyway? Try a drop or two of olive oil or even vegetable oil as an acceptable, practical alternative.

I bet you are wondering if I anoint all of my candles. No, not always. If I am using an unscented tealight, I will occasionally add a drop of essential oil to it for scent. (I use a little dropper to do this—it keeps my hands clean.)

Here is a candle confession for you . . . I work my candle spells primarily with votive candles. I use votives the most because they are inexpensive, come in a wide range of colors, and I can pick them up just about anywhere. I figure that if I am using a scented votive candle in my magick, that's good enough for me. The thought behind my reasoning? Well, the truth is that votive candles have a very high oil content. That's why, as they burn, they turn to liquid wax right away. The high oil content makes the candle highly perfumed and you begin to notice the fragrance of the burning candle immediately.

Also, from a commonsense point of view, not every teen has access to essential oils. Some oils are very expensive and you still have to know which oil to use—for what specific purpose, and on which witchy candle. Are you confused yet? Fear not, my friend. You can skip the oil and just go with the scent already in the candle. As I keep stating, you can find those little babies everywhere: at the grocery store, the department store, and at most arts and crafts supply stores.

So, when faced with the big decision of whether to anoint your spell candles or not, consider the little votive. They have much to offer a practical Witch. Votives are affordable, come in lots of colors and many wonderful, magickal scents. Here is an index of a Witch's dozen (that's thirteen) of common votive candle scents, colors, and their magickal applications.

WITCH'S DOZEN OF SCENTED VOTIVE CANDLES

Apple scented (green or red): Love and healing.

Blueberry scented (blue): Protection.

Cherry scented (dark red): Love.

Cinnamon scented (red): Prosperity, love, and protection.

Cinnamon/spice scented (brown): Happy homes and healthy pets.

Gardenia scented (white): Love, peace, and healing.

Lilac scented (purple): Psychic work, clairvoyance, and faerie magick.

Orange/citrus scented (yellow and orange): Cleansing and refreshing.

Patchouli scented (black): Protection and removing bad luck.

Pine scented (dark green): Prosperity and protection.

Pumpkin scented (orange): Happy homes and harvest.

Rose scented (pink or red): Romance and love.

Vanilla scented (off white): Comforts and calms; encourages love and desire.

Candle Spells

If you are jumping straight into this section without reading the preceding information, you get two Witch demerits. (I have officially raised an eyebrow at you. My hands are on my hips and I am about to launch into a lecture.) Go back and read all of the information on candle color and candle magick. Information and knowledge is power. You want to be powerful? Then study, learn, and absorb the information before you go diving straight into candle spells.

Remember the story about the girl and the bindings from chapter 2? She refused to read the entire magick book, she only skimmed it, because she just wanted the spells. I think we can all safely say, considering her outcome, that it was a pretty stupid thing to do. What do you think is the wisest course of action for you to take? Go on, go back and read all of it.

Thank you, and now our lecture is officially finished.

If you are saying, "Excuse me, I read the information, I even took notes," then I am very proud of you. If you stopped, backed up, and re-read the earlier information, I take away your two demerits and I am proud of you, too. Now, are you ready to experiment, learn, and have a little fun? Great. Here we go!

Focus and Study Spell

This spell uses aromatherapy to help you out. The scent of citrus is clean and refreshing, and the vanilla will help you relax and is comforting. All of those positive emotions are helpful when you have been stressing out over studying for exams and finals. You will still have to study, just think of this as a little extra insurance.

Supplies needed:

- 1 yellow citrus-scented votive candle
- 1 orange citrus-scented votive candle
- 1 off-white, vanilla-scented votive candle
- 3 votive cups
- A lighter or matches
- A safe, flat surface to burn the candles on

Perform any time, day or night. Set up the three candles in a row. Put the vanilla-scented candle in between the orange and yellow ones. Light the candles, then focus your intentions on the outcome that you desire—in this case, doing well on your tests. Repeat the following charm three times:

Yellow and orange flames and magick candles three,
please help me to focus, I have a test this week!
These three candle flames, a symbol of knowledge and power,
will help me to study and learn in this magick hour.

Close the spell by saying,

By all the power of three times three,
as I will it, so shall it be.

I would also add to this spell this closing line:

In no way will this spell reverse
or place upon me any curse.

This last line was written by a famous British Witch named Sybil Leek. It's an excellent little rider to add to the end of any spell. It is also fairly self-explanatory. Let the candles burn while you are studying. You may relight them and reinforce the spell by repeating the charm again. If you are pulling a late-night study session or cramming for finals, let the candles burn until they are consumed.

Healing Spell

Do you have the flu, a virus, or just a nasty cold? How about a walloping case of the blahs? This healing spell will help you get back on your feet. If you'd like, you may set any cold medicines or prescriptions from your doctor next to the candles. Leave them there for a while to give them a little extra magickal boost, to speed up your recovery process.

Supplies:

- 1 blue candle (How about a blueberry-scented one for protecting your health?)

- 1 white candle (Vanilla scented for comfort, or a magnolia scent for healing.)

- 2 candleholders

- A safe, flat surface to burn the candles on

- A lighter or matches

Try working this spell at sunset, when the red, setting sun illuminates the western sky. Use a nail or a large needle to gently scratch the symbol for fire onto the sides of the spell candles. Set the inscribed candle into its holder and you are ready to go. Repeat this charm three times.

As the candle flames dance to the spell I weave,

restore my good health, return my vitality.

My sickness is banished, my fatigue is relieved,

and as I do will it, then so shall it be!

Close the spell. Say,

For the good of all, with harm to none,

by fire and scent, this spell is done.

Let the spell candles burn for one hour every day until you are recovered, repeating the charm every day as you relight the candles. When you are better, if there is any part of the candle left over, light them and let them burn the rest of the way out, or dispose of the leftovers.

Dragon Protection Spell

This spell invokes the fire elementals, the dragons. For this spell you will need a representation of a dragon. This can be a picture, a drawing of your own design, or a little figurine. You will also need to pick up a small, inexpensive piece of jewelry with a dragon on it. This does not have to be elaborate. I am talking tacky, cheap, fun jewelry—you know, the kind of necklaces that you usually see hanging on a black cord? They are displayed and sold by the dozens at festivals and craft shows.

Supplies:

- 1 red, cinnamon-scented candle for protection

- 1 candleholder

- Representation of a dragon

- A dragon charm, necklace, or a ring

- A safe, flat surface to burn the candles on

- A lighter or matches

Time your performance of this spell at the full moon. Check the calendar, many will tell you when the full moons are. So will the Farmer's
Almanac, any of Llewellyn's astrological guides, or the daily newspaper.

Set this spell up facing the south. It is the direction for fire magick
and it's also associated with the dragons. If you have a small picture of
a dragon, place that under the candleholder. If it is a figurine, then
place that off to the side. Set the jewelry on the opposite side of the
candle. Leave the jewelry within reach—you will be picking it up and
putting it on during the spell. Light the candle and say this charm three
times.

> *I call the dragons to come and circle around me,*
>
> *lend me your protection, courage, and your energy.*
>
> (Hold up the jewelry.)
>
> *Now please bless this token with your sacred fire and grace.*
>
> *I am free from all harm, within your sacred space.*

Close the spell. Slip the dragon jewelry on. Say the following line:

> *For the good of all, with harm to none,*
>
> *by the moon and stars, this spell is done.*

Follow this up with a thank-you and farewell to the elementals that
you just called.

> *Hail and farewell, dragons.*
>
> *Many thanks, go in peace.*

Keep the dragon jewelry with you. While you are wearing it, you are
within a protected space. If you cannot wear the jewelry at all times,
try hanging it on your key ring, or stick it into your backpack, purse, or
pocket. You'll think of something. This spell will last from one full
moon phase until the next. If needed, reinforce the spell by doing it
again at the next full moon.

No Candles? No Problem

Now, for those of you who are hyperventilating because you are not allowed to burn candles in your room . . . Relax, I haven't forgotten about you. Here are a few options.

Try burning birthday cake candles instead. They are really inexpensive and they come in lots of colors, including our all-purpose color, white. These candles are consumed within a minute or two. Could you discreetly burn a birthday cake candle in the kitchen without a lot of fuss?

Pour a half cup of salt into a small cup or dish and stick the candle into that. It should hold it up. Light the candle and work the spell. Once the candle has burned out, take the container you used, the salt, and leftover wax with you and leave it on your work space, just as if there were regular burning candles there. The energy is the same whether the candle burns for two minutes or two days.

You can still perform spells without candles. This is not a problem. Can you do glitter? Go to the store and purchase some little tubes of colored glitter. Match the color of the glitter to the candle color that was called for. (You can always use white, it's an all-purpose color.) When it comes to the candle lighting part of your spell, put a small pinch of glitter into your hand.

Call on the element of air for inspiration and the element of fire for transformation; this will speed your spell safely on its way. Then gently blow a small amount of glitter into the air. Or, if you prefer, you can wait until the end of your spell and go outside to blow the glitter to the winds. Again, a small amount of glitter will do, especially if you are working inside. It would not be incredibly subtle to leave piles of glitter all over the carpet.

Finally, you may substitute a live flower for a candle in a spell. Just use a coordinating color of flower, instead of a candle, and focus on that instead. This technique will be discussed in detail later on, in chapter 7.

Candle magick and working with the element of fire is an important part of Witchcraft and natural magick. But, if there was ever a place to warn you once more about burning candles and fire hazards, it would be here. Please, be very careful with the candles. Keep them away from drapes and other flammable materials. Protect them from pets and smaller siblings who could accidentally knock them over. If necessary, let the candles burn inside your shower or bathtub. The kitchen sink is another alternative. How about inside of an unlit fireplace? I use an old cast-iron cauldron to let my larger candles burn safely away in. It keeps the cats away from it and I can set the cauldron on my brick hearth.

Finally, one last gentle reminder. Don't overdo it with dragon energy, okay? Call on them occasionally, not every five minutes. They are an incredible source of power. Fire elementals don't appreciate every Witch and magick user interrupting them and yanking on their tails for a little attention. If you persist, you may discover that you have a rash of electricity problems at home, or the smoke detectors may begin to act up. This is usually the fire elementals' cranky way of telling you to knock it off. Be a wise teenage Witch and work safely with the dragons and candle magick. I am sure you will enjoy much magickal success, prosperity, and health.

Further Reading

Conway, D. J. *Dancing with Dragons* (Llewellyn, 1999).

SIX

The Element of Water

Water, the last of the four natural elements. The magickal element of water represents our emotions, healing, and psychic abilities. Water is found everywhere in our daily lives, from the water you drink, the water in your bathtub, and the rain that falls from the sky. The streams and mighty rivers that cross our continent; a bubbling, fresh spring; the oceans; great lakes; even waterfalls are all a part of the domain of the element of water. Depending on where you live, the element of water affects your life in a variety of ways.

What natural body of water is close to where you live? I live in the Midwest, where the two greatest rivers on the continent, the Mississippi and Missouri Rivers, meet. Here, the rivers are a part of our everyday lives. We drive across them on massive bridges, we keep an eye on them in the spring and watch their flood stages. We do not go swimming in them, at least not around here—their strong and muddy currents are deep and dangerous. I see the rivers almost every day, and my husband's family farms within their floodplains. To me, the rivers are not particularly exciting. I am comfortable with them. To someone else, however, those rivers may stand for adventure and discovery.

When I worked in the historic district of my hometown, I often found myself giving directions to tourists. From a witchy point of view, it was a fun place to work. It also kept me on my toes. The historic district is full of haunted shops and ghosts. Many of the shops are built on top of old cemeteries, where the less wealthy or nonwhite inhabitants were "forgotten" when they moved the cemeteries to higher ground during the 1800s. They discovered this surprising fact in the 1980s when a few shops on Main Street decided to expand and accidentally uncovered graves in the process. Oops! They left the graves where they were and covered them back up with concrete and asphalt. Did I ever see any ghosts when I worked down in the historic district? Yes, I did. But that is another story all in itself.

One day a very nice British gentleman strolled in to ask for a good place to have lunch. He had a great accent and was charming and friendly. Turns out he was also thoroughly lost. He had been strolling along the historic district and the riverfront, snapping pictures and shopping. He was very exciting about being along the riverbanks of the mighty Mississippi, just like his two favorite literary heroes, Tom Sawyer and Huckleberry Finn.

"That's the Missouri River out there," I informed him as I gestured in the general area of the river.

"No, dear," he explained patiently. "I came to see Illinois for the day."

"No, you didn't. You are still in the state of Missouri," I informed him with a grin.

He gave me a polite smile, flashed out his map, and explained patiently how he had driven in from St. Louis to cross the Mississippi River and to see the state of Illinois.

"Honey," I explained, "you just crossed the Missouri River. You are in Missouri, not Illinois."

I gently took the map from him and pointed out where he was on the map. Realization dawned and he was slightly embarrassed. I took his arm and escorted him to an unrestricted view of the riverfront and the park.

"See that river?" I asked. "That's the Missouri River. Lewis and Clark started their expedition from here."

That thrilled him. I directed him to the local museum within the historic district and recommended the haunted restaurant for lunch. He thanked me for my help, told me that my accent was delightful, and was off like a shot. This tourist was so tickled at finding himself "steeped in American history" that he could hardly stand it. To him it was a grand adventure. What it did for me was make me look with new eyes at the river and the town.

So don't turn up your nose at the element of water, however it is found where you live. Whether it's a creek, lakes, rivers, or the ocean, pay attention to natural bodies of water and the local waterways. Get to know their history and respect their life-giving powers.

Water Meditation

Today you and your family are taking a trip to a lake. You have your swimsuit under your clothes and a cooler packed in the trunk of the car, as well as the sunscreen that your mother insisted you take along. You manage to take along your walking stick and you tuck that into the trunk of the car, in case you decide to go exploring later in the day.

Once you arrive at the lake, your family spreads out and settles in. Your younger siblings have already gone screeching and running for the water. After a few moments' hesitation and much internal debate, you chase in after them and indulge in some splashing and scuffling. Then you make your way to a towel and decide to work on your tan. You lay down and relax. A short time later, one of your siblings wakes you up by playfully dumping a pail full of water on you. As you shriek your outrage, the sibling innocently tells you that it's lunchtime and Mom wants you to join the family. With a grumbled threat of retaliation that has the child sticking his tongue out at you, you follow along and go eat your lunch.

After lunch you make good your escape and head out with your walking stick for a nice stroll alone, along the shore of the lake. It's cooler here in the dappled shade. You walk some distance from the family and begin to hum a tune lightly to yourself. You turn a bend in the lake where a small, old, rickety boat dock stretches out into the water. You lean the walking stick against it and inspect the little cove for treasures. You pick up a small shell or two. They are pale white and broken. You root around a little more and find a tiny freshwater clam shell.

It is worn and polished smooth. Then you notice at the base of the shell that a hole has worn through. It would be perfect for hanging on your walking stick.

You walk to the lake's edge to rinse it off. As you walk along the pier, slowly wading into the water, a loud splashing suddenly occurs from under the pier. Startled, you jump back and almost end up falling into the water on your butt. You get out of the water and back onto the shore. Quickly you check around you. There is no one else there. Cautiously you ease your way back to the side of the old boat dock and, bending over slowly, you take a peek under it.

Nothing, just rippling water and old, bleached-out supports. *Must have been a catfish,* you decide, and release your held breath. Relieved, you climb onto the old pier and sit down carefully to tie the shell onto the cords that dangle from the walking stick.

A breeze blows by and you begin to feel extremely lonely. Tears well up and your throat feels tight. *That's weird,* you decide. *I was happy a moment ago.* You swing your feet off of the edge of the boat dock and dangle them into the water. That intense feeling of loneliness returns.

You shut your eyes and try to compose yourself. "What's wrong with me?" you wonder out loud.

"I am lonely. I have no one to talk to . . . " a voice ripples out of nowhere.

Your eyes snap open and you yank your feet up out of the water. The wind has picked up and small waves are slapping against the side of the dock. A familiar sense of dizziness sweeps over you and you realize what is happening. It looks like the last of the four elemental beings has come to pay you a visit. Dearly hoping that the water elemental will not be a Loch Ness monster type of creature, you sit still and wait.

Suddenly there is a splash behind you and a weight comes down onto the dock. You flinch and turn around to find a young woman has appeared behind you. She has splashed you with water and is leaning her crossed arms on the dock. She tips her head over to the side and smiles gently at you.

"Hello." You offer a cautious greeting as you turn around to face her.

She has very long, dark hair that completely drapes over her. She regards you with a friendly expression and for a split second you think that this might be an ordinary person playing a prank on you, until you look into the woman's eyes. They are a luminous shade of green—an intense, glowing green-blue unlike any color you have ever seen. You look down at her to see if anything else is unusual. She appears to look pretty normal to you, besides the fact that she is naked. It's a good thing that her hair is so long, you think to yourself, and struggle not to be embarrassed.

You hear a silvery laugh and feel amusement shimmer around you, but the laugh you heard is coming from inside your head. The water spirit is not speaking out loud. Her laugher continues to echo merrily through your head as you smile back at her.

"Oh, I get it," you say.

"Greetings," she tips her head and studies you just as thoroughly as you did her. "What do you have wrapped around you?" She tugs at the swimsuit with a frown.

"That's a swimsuit," you tell her. "People wear them when they go swimming."

For her answer, you feel a ripple of amusement as she raises her arms to show you that she does not wear one.

"Yeah, yeah, I see," you look quickly around, hoping no one else can see her. She smiles indulgently at you and then shakes her head and tosses her hair to cover herself.

"You must be an undine, right?" you ask.

For an answer, you feel a jolt of pride and pleasure course through you.

"Have you always lived here?" you ask her.

For an answer, you receive images inside your mind. You see the fish and animals who make their home in and around the lake. You see the lake as it is now and as it was many years ago. Next, you are shown the countless sunrises and sunsets the undine has experienced. You see the lake in the grips of winter, completely frozen over. You are shown the lake in the spring and during high summer. Lastly, you see the lake as it is during the fall. Your senses sharpen as you envision the golden and russet-colored trees. You smell the crisp air and watch the changing leaves drift gently to the surface of the lake. The air is filled with the cries of the migratory birds who take refuge here before continuing their journey south. Faster and faster, one image follows after the next. The images are going so fast, you can barely differentiate between them. A cool hand rests on your leg and the images suddenly stop.

Overwhelmed, you let out a shaky breath. Suddenly cold, despite the sun beating down on you, you hug your knees for warmth. "What do you have to teach me?" you ask her.

"Water is the element of emotion and intuition," her voice shimmers through your mind. "The element of water can bring about healing and cleansing." She raises her hands and clear water trickles from them.

"Water may be used to see the past or divine the future, if you care to try." She now cups her hands together and then slowly opens them to reveal the black, glistening water that she now holds within. Incredibly, a full moon and dozens of stars reflect off of the captured water's midnight surface.

"What do you see?" her voice echoes inside your head.

As you look within her cupped hands, you see yourself as a toddler holding onto your parents as you took your first steps. You feel your delight and their pride in you. You recall the feeling of being held and soothed as a little child when you fell down and skinned your knees. It makes you grin as you look back at the "magic" power of a Band-Aid and how, with a kiss, your hurts were made all better. The emotions rocket through you and you look with wonder at the undine.

The undine nods her head at you and the water flows out through her hands and back into the lake. She gives you a moment to compose yourself and then her mind tells yours, "The creatures identified with the element of water are the whale, the dolphin, and the fish."

Suddenly, the water within the cove is alive with movement. The surface of the water shimmers and boils with hundreds of fish that seem to roll over each other and try to break the surface at the same time. Enchanted, you reach down and run your fingers along the backs of the swirling fish. Then, with a graceful gesture from the undine, the water smooths out and the fish swim away as the little cove becomes calm again.

Now she reaches up to your walking stick and sends the shell, feathers, and the holey stone hanging from the cords on a lazy spin. She lifts up the newly acquired shell. "This is one of the symbols for the element of water," she nods at you. "Here is another." She draws a symbol on the dock with her wet fingers. It is a triangle with one point down.

"But that is so simple," you say with a frown.

"There are times when simple is best," her voice reverberates through your mind.

"How about this?" You draw waves on the dock as she did, next to her triangle.

The undine looks up at you patiently. "Yes, this would be an elemental symbol as well."

"This is so cool!" you say. "Can I ask how you did that trick with the water. . .?" you trail off as you hear your name being shouted. You turn your head, irritated at the interruption. The dock shifts as she eases down from the side.

"Don't go yet," you ask her as she lowers herself back into the water.

She looks at you solemnly and intently, as if she is trying to memorize your features. "I must go now." She glides smoothly through the water and out farther away from you.

You look over your shoulder—any minute now and your family will turn the corner. You jump to your feet to see her better. You quickly jog to the end of the boat dock. "I just wanted to say thank you," you call quietly after her.

She stops and turns to look at you. For a moment you feel her delight in having had the chance to "talk" to you. For her, it was quite the adventure.

"Remember what I have shown you," her voice sounds sweetly in your mind. The undine gives you a sassy smile and then disappears under the water with a humongous splash that she aims right at you. With nowhere to go, you stand there and let it nail you.

You laugh and wipe the water out of your eyes. You look out at the lake. It is smooth and calm, like she was never there. But you know better. Dripping, you retrieve your walking stick. You call out to your family that you are on your way and then, making your way to the end of the dock, you jump back onto the shore.

You stop and touch the shell that you added to your other treasures and admire your walking stick. It has seen you through many adventures and now it carries a symbol of each of the four elements. The holey stone represents the element of earth; your feathers, dangling from the cords, for the element of air; the dragon-shaped burn mark on the staff symbolizes fire; and lastly, your little freshwater shell stands for water. Turning, you look back to the lake one final time, then you wave to your family and walk to meet them as they make the final curve into the cove.

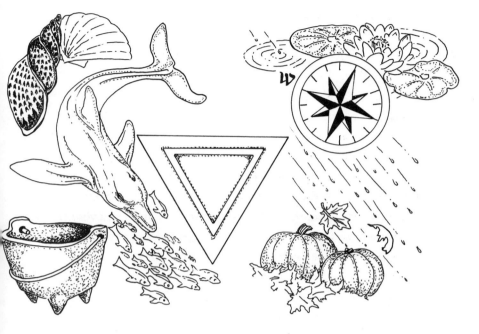

WATER CORRESPONDENCE CHART

Direction: West

Color: Blue

Time of Day: Sunset

Season of the Year: Autumn

Places: Rivers, lakes, ponds, springs, streams, the ocean

Witch's Tool: Cup or cauldron

Deities: Aphrodite, Nimue (Lady of the Lake), Oshun the Yoruban river goddess, Poseidon, Triton, and Yemaya

Symbol: ▽

Animals: Whales, dolphins, and fish

Elemental Beings: Undines, sirens, and mermaids

Magicks Include: Love, emotions, healing, and prophecy

Natural Representations Include:

- Seashells

- Water-smoothed pebbles

- And, of course, water

A Little Information on the Water Elementals

The undines are the elemental beings associated with water, rivers, and streams. Typically undines are thought to be female, and very sensual and luxurious. The undines are sweet, gentle, and shy. They are the spirits of freshwater lakes, ponds, springs, rivers, and streams. The undines can help you enhance your psychic abilities, if you wish. Just don't expect the spirit of the undine to follow you home. Legend says that they can never venture too far from their water's edge, as they are bound to the body of water that they inhabit and protect.

The historic siren and the mermaid are most often associated with the sea or ocean. The very word *siren* is classically used to describe a female who is alluring or who possesses an amazing singing voice. The siren was thought to be very sexual and seductive; they were often described as having the upper body of a woman and the lower torso of a bird, from the thighs down. The sirens in Greek mythology were sometimes associated with Artemis, Athena, Hera, and Dionysus.

Sirens were thought to be beautiful and dangerous, like the sea itself. Mythology warns of sirens luring men to their deaths by distracting them with their singing and causing their boats to crash along the rocks. In addition to causing the deaths of hapless sailors, the sirens and their power of song may also have characterized the joy and exhilaration of music, or even of various animal powers (as they were half bird).

The mermaid has many of the same qualities as the siren. The mermaid, however, seems to have an extra dash of romance thrown in to soften her image. Mermaids could also lure men into drowning, or they could fall in love with them and save them as well. There are tales of men taking sea spirits as wives in many cultures. The mermaid leaves her sea life behind and takes on a human form. Sometimes these marriages lasted happily for years, but many of these tales end sadly, for the sea spirit-wife never fits into the human world. Sometimes she is misunderstood or even mistreated. Then she returns to the sea, leaving her husband and family behind.

Communicating with the Water Spirits

If you want to gain the attention of the gentler undines, you may try placing a small posy or bouquet of flowers at the water's edge for them. You may also float a few blossoms on the water as well. The undines are beautiful, feminine, and will communicate with you while you are in their realm, through your emotions. You may feel overcome with emotion or get giddy and excited. Has this ever happened to you?

The first time I stood on the shores of Lake Michigan, I was completely overwhelmed. A friend had taken me to her home state of Michigan for a garden sight-seeing trip. She stopped along the way at a shoreside town so that I could see a lighthouse and finally get to see the Great Lakes. I sat, frozen, in the car for a moment, absolutely amazed at how big the lake really was. Grinning at my reaction, my friend pulled the car into a park by the lakeside and turned me loose to go and see the lighthouse and, of course, so I could get my feet into the water.

I couldn't get over how deep blue the water was, all of the trees along the shores and how the lake smelled. The sight of all that fresh water blew me away. Who knew it was going to be so fabulously huge?

As I stood there, tears welled up and my throat felt tight. I knew that the water spirits were there with me in that place. How could they not be? As we walked along the shoreline, I picked up a small piece of driftwood, thinking that it might make a nice wand someday. I silently thanked the spirits of the lake and have held that memory close ever since.

I guess if you grew up along the ocean you get over the fascination and amazement of its size and power. For those of us who have only seen them once or twice, it is a truly magickal experience. While on an anniversary trip to Salem, Massachusetts, my husband and I drove down to Cape Cod for the afternoon to see the Atlantic Ocean. We ate lunch and did some shopping in Provincetown, where a shop clerk directed us to a picturesque beach where we could walk and take some pictures.

Being a couple of semi-grownup kids from the Midwest, we took one look at that ocean and then raced each other to the shoreline. It was early April and cold on the beach. The fact that we had winter coats on and the other people out jogging or walking the beach thought we were nuts didn't matter in the slightest to us. We had to get in the water.

Who else but a couple of tourists would toss their shoes, roll up their pant legs, and race in to go wading when it was freezing outside? We spent a few hours sitting on the boulders along the beach, taking pictures and gathering tiny shells and smooth pebbles. Perching on those boulders, watching the green waves splash and then turn to lacy foam, was awe inspiring. I sat there and basked in the slowly warming sunlight, trying to get a feel for the Atlantic Ocean—to really sense it.

In a place like that, it was easy to imagine mermaids singing and sea creatures sliding in and out of the emerald-colored waves. I opened my purse to look at the little papier-mâché mermaid figurine that I had just bought while shopping. Her tag said she was a "Sea Goddess." She had wild golden hair and her fin was painted a metallic gold. *Mermaids and the ocean,* I thought to myself as I tucked her safely away, *seem to be the order of the day.*

As my husband dropped down on the sand to finally put his shoes back on, I commented that I felt like a mermaid perched up on the rocks, and he smiled over at me. Suddenly he jumped up, tossed his socks and shoes aside, raced for the water, and went in up to his knees.

"What are you doing?" I laughed at him, as he made a grab for something in the water.

He waded back to me, dripping wet and holding a huge, open clamshell. He was grinning like a maniac.

"Look at this!" he said triumphantly.

The shell was completely open and smooth and white. Both halves of the shell were unbroken and polished. Was it the prettiest shell we'd ever seen? No, but it was one humongous shell and we accepted it as a gift from the ocean and the water spirits. I guess the mermaids must have heard me. We drove back to Salem that afternoon to the bed-and-breakfast where we were staying, a little damp, but revved up from our afternoon on the chilly beach. That large clamshell now sits on my mantle in the living room, to remind us of the water spirits and of a wonderful afternoon adventure.

Mermaids and sirens, like dragons, are powerful nature spirits, and I would be carefully respectful and not invoke too much of their energy. Their gifts often come with a price. Remember that the element of water is associated with our emotions and psychic abilities. So if you go overboard with water spirit energy, you may notice that you are more emotional—you may go on crying jags and have your feelings hurt very easily. If that happens, ground yourself. Take a walk outside and reconnect to the earth. You may also try fanning a little incense smoke over your body; it will help clear out any extra sadness or hurt feelings. This technique is called smudging; it is a psychic form of cleansing that works in harmony with the element of air.

Don't panic about these water spirits, now, they aren't lurking about or waiting to get you. As the undines are gentler water spirits than their oceanic sisters, working with the undines is probably your safest bet. If you live along the coast and feel more of a connection to the mermaids and the sirens, then you should instinctively know to show them the respect that they deserve. After all, if you live close to the ocean, you are already very aware of how capricious and powerful an entity the ocean truly is. If you are cautious of the mermaids' and sirens' elemental power and show them both respect and good manners, you should get along just fine.

Scrying in Water

Scrying is the art of gaining psychic knowledge by looking into a reflective surface, such as water. Traditionally a cup, bowl, or shallow container of water is employed. This water-filled scrying vessel was often blessed by catching the reflection of the moon on its surface. To do this, simply hold up your container full of water and angle it to reflect the moon for a few moments. Be careful not to dump the water on yourself. The first time I tried to do this, I was so busy trying to lift and lower the bowl so I could catch the moon's reflection, I ended up spilling the entire contents of the bowl all over myself!

Oh, well, it gave me a good laugh, and I relaxed and enjoyed the idea instead of stressing out over it. I suspect the water spirits were trying to tell me to loosen up and enjoy the process, instead of thinking it to death. If you are limited to working indoors, go with a cup, bowl, or small cauldron full of water.

However, since we are going for the theme of natural magick, try working outdoors. Take your container of water outside with you on the porch or patio and settle in. Or work with a natural source of water instead. Any natural body of water may be used to perform a scrying. You could use a lake, tidal pool, a stream, a river, or even a backyard swimming pool—just as long as the water reflects.

Timing: A good time to work a scrying is in the early evening, before it gets too dark outside. We want to avoid the glare of the sun off the water, but we don't want you skulking around in the dark. Oh, and don't worry about blessing an outdoor source of water. It already has the reflected energies of both the moon and the sun within it.

Directions: Sit down and get comfortable. If you are outdoors, then sit securely and safely down alongside the body of water. We do not want to be so busy leaning over to look that we fall in. So if you do not swim well, sit by the shallows, okay? Alternatively, if you are indoors, set the container of water within easy reach. If you are stuck indoors, you may want to light a few candles and dim the other lights in the room; it will help to put you in a magickal mood.

Ground and center yourself. Take three deep, slow, and even breaths. Decide what it is you would like to know about. Do you wish information on a future event? Or are you just looking to see? Try looking into your past, and ask to see a happy time when you were a child. (If you recall, this was the undine's gift during the water meditation.) Now gaze into the water and let your mind drift. Try this scrying charm to aid your endeavor.

The gift of the undines I ask now for me,

draw upon my emotions, help me to see.

Grant me the gift of prophecy and second sight,

show me the future, present, and the past, this night.

Usually, in about five minutes, images should start to appear within your mind or you may actually see them in the surface of the water. The water is merely a tool that helps you focus. It's sort of like those 3-D pictures where you have to let your eyes slowly become unfocused to see the 3-D image. You may receive only impressions at first, and you may feel lots of emotions. Allow yourself to blink naturally, it is not a staring contest. Give yourself twenty minutes or so for your first attempt at scrying and see what happens.

Closing: After you are finished, thank the water spirits for their help. Try using the Nature Spirits Charm in chapter 3, on page 50. If you had your scrying water in a container, return it to the earth. Pour it onto the ground or down the drain. If you didn't have any luck with your first attempt at scrying, don't worry. It takes a little practice. Next time, try performing a scrying on the night of a full moon. The full moon is thought to be a time of increased psychic powers and magick. That should help you to have more success.

Three Flowers in a Fountain Spell

Here is a peaceful and strengthening water spell. Use this spell for those times when you feel intimidated or afraid. It will help bolster your courage and increase your confidence. For this spell, you need to find a fountain. Instead of tossing coins in, try floating a few flowers or small blossoms on the water instead.

Supplies:

- 3 small flowers or blossoms, any color

- A fountain

Do this spell any time. Stand or sit next to the fountain. Dip your fingers into the water and imagine that all of your fears and worries are being washed away. Let the water absorb your troubles and take them away from you. Shake the water off your fingers and pick up the flowers. You may say the charm silently in your head or quietly out loud. If you are discreet and quiet, no one should notice anything that you are doing.

These flowers I hold within my hands will bring me peace and love.

Great Goddess, smile down upon me with your blessings from above.

(Drop the flowers in the water.)

I ask for serenity, send me courage and the strength of the mountains,

I cast this tranquil spell as these flowers float gently within the fountain.

Close the spell. Look at the flowers bobbing happily in the water. Then say,

By all the powers of three times three,

as I will it, so shall it be.

Ground and center yourself. Now, turn and walk away from your fears; leave them behind you. Don't look back.

Honoring Your Favorite Element

As we finish up these chapters on the magick of the elements, I want you to stop for a moment and congratulate yourself on everything that you have learned so far. Do you have a preferred element? Why do you suppose it has become your favorite? Take a moment and jot it down in the space provided below. Now, list all the reasons why this is your favorite element. When you are finished with that, come up with a way to honor this element each day.

For example, if water is your favorite, then ask for a cleansing or a blessing from a water deity every time you take a bath. Become more aware of the life-giving qualities of water as you water the plants in the yard or the houseplants that are growing inside. That's simple enough. Then take a look at the remaining three elements and figure out a way to incorporate something from those into your daily life as well.

For fire, you could stop and acknowledge the power of the sun. Or, as you light a candle, notice just how much illumination one tiny flame can bring into a dark room. How do you think working with the element of fire can bring illumination into your life?

Acknowledging the element of air could be as simple as enjoying the refreshing breeze as it blows by. Celebrate all of the change that the element of air can bring. To honor the element of earth, maybe you could work on your sense of responsibility by working in the yard and planting some flowers. Volunteer to help clean up a park or other natural area. Or, if you don't have a yard but yearn to "dig in" to plants, then purchase a small houseplant—something easy to tend to, like an ivy or philodendron—and then take good care of it.

Think of all the spells, charms, and natural magick that you have discovered already. Consider all of the ways you have discovered of looking around you and seeing things in nature as if for the first time. Exciting, isn't it? You have plenty of reasons to be proud of yourself. Well done! Now you are learning to look at nature and the world around you with a Witch's heart and with a Witch's mind.

Further Reading

Cunningham, Scott. *Earth, Air, Fire & Water* (Llewellyn, 1991).

Cunningham, Scott. *Earth Power* (Llewellyn, 1983).

A PLACE FOR YOUR THOUGHTS ON THE ELEMENTS

A PLACE FOR YOUR THOUGHTS ON THE ELEMENTS

A PLACE FOR YOUR THOUGHTS ON THE ELEMENTS

A PLACE FOR YOUR THOUGHTS ON THE ELEMENTS

III
Looking Deeper into Natural Magick

It is only with the **HEART**
that one can see rightly;
What is **ESSENTIAL**
is **INVISIBLE** to the eye.

—ANTOINE DE SAINT-EXUPERY

SEVEN

The Magick of Flowers and Trees

The folklore and mythology of plants is a bewitching topic that I could go on and on about. However, I will restrain myself and keep things easy and uncomplicated for you. This chapter definitely will make you look at the flowers and trees that you see everyday in a whole new light. I will introduce you to some of the techniques of magickal herbalism, which is the art of performing magick with various plants, herbs, and flowers. Did you know that plants themselves have their own magickal qualities and elemental associations? These natural elemental energies are just waiting to be noticed and utilized.

Now, before you start imagining gothic, exotic plants and roots like wolfsbane and mandrake (which are both very toxic, by the way), put your broom in neutral and just hover with me for a while. Magickal plants are all around you and they are much easier to find than you probably think. I'll give you a hands-on type of example. You'll need to broom yourself outside for a moment.

Do you notice any annual geraniums planted in pots, window boxes, and containers in your neighborhood? Would you be surprised to know that those humble, everyday flowers have a strong magickal significance? Geraniums are aligned to the element of water. The geranium flower represents protection and safe homes. Geraniums come in a wide variety of colors, and—just like in candle magick—the different colors have their own magickal uses.

Red geraniums are protective and ward off negative influences. When they are planted in window boxes or placed in pots by the front door, they strengthen a home's security. White geraniums are for peace and fertility, pink geraniums are for love and affection, and coral-colored geraniums encourage energy and strength. If you notice ivy or vinca vines planted in the containers with the geraniums, these green foliage plants add more protection and inspire fidelity to the magickal mix.

Here is another charming example that you probably overlook every spring. Go check out the grass in your lawn—can you find any violets? Remember when you were little and you picked your mom bouquets of these tiny, purple-blue flowers? The violet is a dainty wildflower that, when used in magick, promotes love and protection. It is also a favorite faerie flower.

Now that you are starting to pay attention to the plants that are around you, I want you to take a good look at the trees growing in your neighborhood. Watch for pine trees and maples, those are easy to identify. Do you see any of those? In magickal herbalism, pine needles can be utilized in prosperity and protection spells. Maple leaves are used in magick to sweeten things up and to promote love and harmony.

Would you like some more backyard magick examples? How about enchanting trees like the oak and the cypress? Or ornamental flowering trees and shrubs such as dogwoods, magnolias, and the lilac? You may find it interesting to know that the beloved oak is a symbol for the God, and often marks the place of a magickal sanctuary. The cypress is a tree of mystery, magick, and protection. The beautiful dogwood protects both the property that it is planted on and the family who lives there. The flowering magnolia encourages beauty and hospitality, while the fragrant lilac shrub is protective and a faerie favorite. The scent of lilacs actually helps promote cleansing and clairvoyance, and also increases psychic ability—and these are just a few examples of magickal plants.

Nature is sacred, and the supplies that you need for natural magick are to be found growing all around you. How about those apples? Oh, and by the way—the apple tree is a powerful magickal tree. The foliage, blooms, and the fruit of the apple tree are incorporated into spells for faerie magick, love, and happy homes. Magickal plants really are everywhere.

Working with Flowers in Magick

There are two ways to look at flower magick. One is to work with the traditional magickal correspondences of each plant, and the other is to use the flower as a sort of living candle in a spell. Let's say for some reason you either could not locate a yellow candle for a study spell or were not allowed to burn one. No problem. Enter the garden Witch. You may use a flower as a substitute for a burning candle in natural magick. How about exchanging the candle for a complementary yellow flower, like a daisy, and tucking it into a vase? The daisy stands for cheerfulness and innocence. The color yellow is complementary to the element of air, knowledge, study, and intellectual pursuits. Set it up where you can enjoy the flower, and go ahead and work the spell. Just use the flower to focus on instead of the candle. It will work out just as well.

All-Purpose Flower Charm

In this enchanted time and bewitching hour,

I call upon the magick within this flower.

By color and scent this flower charm is begun,

As I will, so must it be, and let it harm none!

If this idea appeals to you, refer to the color magick chart below and match the color of the flower to the chart. (You will notice that this chart is almost identical to the candle color chart from chapter 5. It is listed here so you won't have to go searching for it again.) The only difference in working with a flower instead of a candle is that the flower does not burn out; instead, it fades. Watch your flower in the vase and when it starts to wither and fade, you need to dispose of it. You may either throw it away, add it to a compost pile, or leave it neatly outside for nature to reclaim.

COLORS AND FLOWER MAGICK

Red: Love, healing, protection, and the Mother Goddess.

Orange: Energy, enthusiasm, and intensity.

Yellow: Creativity, communication, study, and the God.

Green: Prosperity, herbal magick, healing, and the Green Man.

Blue: Peace, spirit, and rejuvenation.

Purple: Personal power, psychic work, and faerie magick.

Pink: Love, magick for children, and friendship.

White: All-purpose, defense, harmony, and the Maiden Goddess.

Black/Dark Burgundy: Removing negativity, breaking bad luck, and the Crone Goddess.

The other technique of floral magick is based on the language of flowers. An example of this floral language that you may already be aware of is that red roses signify both love and passion. The white rose symbolizes new beginnings and an innocent, pure love (which is why white roses are so popular as a bridal flower). In the language of flowers, there is a symbolic meaning for each bloom or different type of foliage. These definitions of the flowers, plants, and trees are based on the older folklore and the legends surrounding them. Indeed, each separate tree and flower has an enchanting message for you. Learning about the language of flowers is a fun and easy way to understand which flowers and foliage are to be used for which type of magick.

Easy-to-Find Magickal Flowers

Finding magickal flowers to add to your spells and charms is simple enough. What do you have blooming in the garden at home? Is there anything blooming in pots and containers on your deck or balcony? See what you can scrounge up. However, don't use this as an excuse to snitch some flowers from the park or from your neighbor. Be polite. The Goddess and the God won't turn a blind eye to your pilfering. Your spell will probably backfire if you go around stealing supplies. Once again, recall the Rule of Three: *Whatever you give out returns to thee . . .*

If nothing is available to you at home, then consider these common-sense suggestions. A single carnation, mum, or daisy from the florist can come in many colors and they are inexpensive to work with. Try asking your neighbor for a bloom or two from their garden. Or you could go and buy the blooming plant from the nursery to plant in your own yard, or in a pot for your windowsill or deck.

In the following list I have made every effort to give you the names of flowers that are both easy to locate and identify. If the names of some of these flowers are not familiar to you, ask the people who work at the garden center or the florist to show you which ones they are. Also, check out the library for books on flowers, or surf the Internet. Look for gardening sites with plant photos.

While you are at the nursery or garden center looking around, take a peek at the signs and the little plant identification tags that are included in the pots of the ready-to-plant flowers. If the tags say they are annuals, that means the plant will complete its growing cycle within one year. As soon as frost and winter hits, it will wither and decline. A plant that is listed as a perennial will go dormant during the winter months, then grow again and rebloom the following season. Those small plant tags will not only identify the blooming plant for you, but they will also tell you how and where to plant it for the best results.

THE GARDEN WITCH'S LIST OF COMMON MAGICKAL FLOWERS

Aster: These perennial purple-blue daisylike flowers will bloom in late summer-early fall, and the flowers are utilized in charms and spells to promote love. Its elemental correspondence is water. The aster was a popular flower often used to honor the Greek gods. (Hint: butterflies love these flowers.)

Begonia: A popular blooming annual. In the language of flowers, the begonia means "warning." Plant this pretty and versatile sun- and shade-loving annual in pots and containers for protection.

I associate this perky little plant with the element of earth for its hardy and practical qualities.

Carnation: My favorite florist's flower. Carnations come in a rainbow of colors and they are inexpensive. Usually a single carnation will cost $1.00 to $1.50 per stem. The scent of carnations encourages health and vitality, which explains their fire elemental connection. The magickal correspondences change with the many meanings of the flower.

Red: Love, passion, and healing.

Pink: Maternal love, beauty, and best friends.

Yellow: Friendship and happiness.

Orange: Energy and vitality.

Purple: Passion and mystery.

White: Peace, protection, and love.

Red and white striped: "A refusal."

Got an old flame that keeps coming back around? Try working with a striped carnation. Here is a quick flower spell to get that old flame to move along.

The "Moving On" Spell

Supplies:

- One red-and-white-striped carnation from the florist

- A bud vase, filled with water

- A small pot or container planted full of purplish-blue pansies

- An item in sympathy with the person, such as a photo, or a sample of their handwriting

Perform at sunset. We want to utilize the closing energies of the day. Set the striped carnation in the vase and place the container of pansies next to it. Set your item of sympathy between the flowers. Remember that this spell intends no harm. It is simply a way to encourage both the old flame and yourself to move along to happier things. Repeat the following charm three times.

Carnation with stripes of bright red and white,

lend your power, assist me in my plight.

Back away and move on, old boyfriend/girlfriend of mine,

be happy with someone else, come rain or shine.

Magick pansies with your faces so bright and blue,

help me to feel safe and strong in all that I do.

Close the spell. Say,

For the good of all, with harm to none,

by the moon and stars, this spell is done.

When the carnation fades, dispose of it. Set your pot of pansies outside in a semi-shady spot and enjoy their perky faces and the healing energy they send to you. Now, get rid of the old mementos from this past relationship, will you? Why are you keeping those things? Chuck the photo or handwriting sample from the spell into the garbage can. By removing all of these old items from your life, you help to break the emotional ties that bound you together. Carry them right outside and into the garbage can. Brush off your hands and announce,

This spell is sealed.

Chrysanthemum: Chrysanthemums are protective perennial flowers and are rumored to keep ghosts away from your home. They have the elemental correlation of fire. They are available in almost every color—red, burgundy, purple, orange, yellow, and even a brown-bronze tone. That makes choosing the right one for color magick a snap! A favorite fall flower, you may set a few pots of these with your pumpkins on Samhain/Halloween to protect your property. In the language of flowers, red mums mean love, yellow mums bring cheerfulness, and white mums invoke truth.

Daffodil: The yellow daffodil is a symbol of spring. The daffodil brings luck and joy into your life. This flowering bulb belongs to the element of water. In the language of flowers, the daffodil symbolizes chivalry and honor.

Daisy: The daisy is a symbol of youth, innocence, and cheer. The daisy also comes in a wide variety of colors, and is another inexpensive flower available year-round from the florist. The elemental associations of the daisy are both air (for freshness and spring) and water (for love and emotions). The white daisy always reminds me of the Maiden Goddess and brides. Choose the daisy color carefully to coordinate with your magickal need. (Refer to the flower color magick chart, page 128.)

Geranium: In the opening of this chapter, the geranium's magickal qualities were discussed. However, in the language of flowers, the red geranium says, "You have bewitched me!" The white geranium's message is, "You are graceful," and the pink geranium denotes preference.

Honeysuckle: The honeysuckle is a favorite old-fashioned blooming garden shrub. Its elemental correspondence is earth. Magickally, honeysuckle foliage and blooms are used to promote prosperity. In the language of flowers it bespeaks of a devoted friend.

Hyacinth: The hyacinth is one of my favorite fragrant spring bulbs. They are available in colors ranging from white and pinks to blues and purples. This bulb is connected with the element of water. In aromatherapy, the scent of the hyacinth promotes relaxation and a good night's sleep. If you are grieving or have a case of the blues, the hyacinth is the flower to work with. Magickally, this flower brings love and peace.

Hydrangea: The hydrangea is a shade-loving blooming shrub. In my garden, the huge pale blue and purple-colored round blooms usually appear in July. They slowly change in color to a green and then, as the temperature changes in the fall, they are blushed with a dusky red. If you prune the blooms carefully it will not hurt the shrub. Just limit yourself to one or two blooms. (Just a couple of these mop-head hydrangea blooms can fill up an entire vase.) In magick, the hydrangea is a protective plant. Either work with the flowers, or in the winter a small amount of bark from the dormant stems may be used for protection and, if necessary, hex breaking. I suspect that all of the elements are complementary to the hydrangea. In the language of flowers, the hydrangea bloom symbolizes devotion.

Iris: The multihued iris is the sacred flower of the Greek goddess Iris. She was the messenger of the gods and her symbol was the rainbow. The iris is a perennial and is widely available in almost every color of the rainbow, even black. The iris is a regal and beautiful flower that is associated with the element of water. In floral languages, the blue iris stands for a message. That's pretty appropriate, don't you think? A red iris means passion, and a yellow iris represents both enthusiasm and desire. The mysterious black iris seems to whisper to us of an enchantment. Use the iris in spells designed for communication and for confidence.

Jasmine: This delicate flower signifies joy. The jasmine flower is associated with the moon and the Goddess. In magick, the scent of jasmine is used to promote clairvoyance and prophetic dreams. It aligns with the element of water. The flowers themselves are carried to draw money and prosperity to you.

Lily: The perennial lily has a long magickal history. The lily is a symbol of the archangel Gabriel and is a sacred flower to many goddesses, including Lilith, Nephthys, Venus, Kwan Yin, and Mary. The elemental correspondence of this flower is water. The many different colors of the lily all have separate definitions.

White: Majesty and purity.

Yellow: Excitement.

Orange Tiger Lily: Love and passion.

Deep Red: This lily is sacred to the goddess Lilith and symbolizes strength and a strong will.

Deep Pink: The intensely fragrant Stargazer lily, also called *rubrum*, may be used to invoke the magick of the faeries and nature spirits. It is believed that the faeries enjoy sweet, strongly scented flowers, and this one definitely fits the bill.

Marigold: The common marigold has quite a lot of magickal history behind it. It is a symbol of the sun, and in the language of flowers it stands for health, constancy, and affection. The marigold corresponds with the element of fire. This perky annual flower holds up to the intense heat of long summers and cheerfully blooms away. Work with the happy marigold to encourage a joyous and healthy life.

Pansy: The pansy has the folk name of "heartsease." The pansy helps ease your depression after a break-up, which is why it was worked into the Moving On Spell, listed above. This flower is sacred to the Greco-Roman god Eros/Cupid. It also belongs to the element of

water. The pansy's sunny face conveys cheer and loving vibrations. In the language of flowers, the pansy invites you to have
happy thoughts. Pansies can bloom happily in cooler weather.
They are annuals and are at their happiest when planted in the
early spring or fall. Pansies do not tolerate the summer heat.

Rose: The queen of flowers, the rose is a famous symbol for love. Its
elemental correspondence, like so many other flowers, is water. In
magick, a rose is used to bring love, and the petals are often used
in charm bags and spells to "speed things up." The many different
colors of the rose have their own unique meanings.

Red: "I love you."

White: New beginnings, pure and innocent love.

Red and white: Creativity and solidarity.

Yellow: Joy and happiness.

Coral: "I admire you."

Orange: Vitality and energy.

Pink: Beauty and elegance.

Peach: Charm.

Purple: Power and passion.

Ivory: Romance and a steadfast, mature love.

Snapdragon: The snapdragon has the elemental association of—you
guessed it—fire. The annual snapdragon can be grown in the garden as a spell-breaking magickal flower. Snaps, as they are sometimes called, are used in magick for protection and to help keep
manipulative influences away from you. The snapdragon is also
available at most florists and is a tall and sturdy flower to work
with. Snaps come in a gorgeous variety of colors. With all the
snap colors to choose from, you can easily specialize and use the
color that is best suited to your spellwork.

Sunflower: The sunflower has been honored throughout history as a sun symbol. The people of ancient times were very fond of this flower, as they noticed that the flower turned to face the sun throughout the day. The elemental association for this flower is fire. The magickal uses for the bright and cheerful sunflower are fame, granting wishes, and happiness. In the language of flowers, the sunflower says, "I think of you with admiration."

Tulip: The bouncy spring tulip brings good luck and protects against poverty. It is aligned to the element of earth. There are a dozen or so different floral language definitions for the tulip. As before, the different colors have their own special meanings. However, with the tulip, all of the definitions revolve around love.

Red: Undying love; "I will love you forever."

Pink: Dreaminess and imagination; "dream lover."

Pale Green and White Mixture: "I am a jealous lover."

Yellow: "I am hopelessly in love with you."

White: A faraway love; "Return to me."

Variegated: "You have beautiful eyes."

Maroon-Black: A loving enchantment; "the magick of the night."

Zinnia: The colorful zinnia is a great flower to grow from seed. It is a reliable bloomer and it attracts many species of butterflies. To me, because of the butterflies, the elemental correspondence of this flower would be air. In the language of flowers, the zinnia signifies a faraway friend. In the earth element chapter, the zinnia was a suggested ingredient of the Drawing Friendship Spell. A zinnia is an outstanding flower to use as a substitute for a candle in a spell, as it is available in many colors and sizes. Pick up a package of seeds this spring and try planting some zinnias for your family. Not only will they give you lots of bright-colored blooms for both flower arrangements and to enjoy in the garden, but the show the butterflies will provide is well worth the minimal cost of a few packages of seeds.

The Mystic Language of Trees

The language of flowers encompasses more than just perky flowers in terra cotta pots and traditional gardens. Now, if flowers just aren't your thing, but you really like trees, you should enjoy this next section. Trees have been revered since ancient times. This is easy to understand, as a tree can live for much longer than a person's life span. The Druids, wisewomen, and cunning men all held trees to be sacred. There was even a tree designated to each month of the old Celtic year. In chapter 4 you learned of the faerie trinity of trees. This trio of magickal trees is the oak, the ash, and the thorn (hawthorn). Whatever place these three trees were found growing together was thought to have been an enchanted place—a sort of gateway to the Faerie realm.

Have you ever talked to a tree? Well, why haven't you? We depend on our trees to help clean the air and to make more oxygen for everyone to breathe on this planet. Nature and human life are interconnected. A tree can be considered a sort of bridge between the earth and the sky. The whole point in learning natural magick is to teach you to become more aware of and tuned in to your natural surroundings. If you have never "talked" to the trees, then you are missing out on something very special. Would you like to try your hand at meeting a tree spirit and getting to know the life force that is inherent in every tree? I thought you might. This is a fun and simple magickal exercise. It is easy to perform and it will not take up much of your time.

Communicating with the Spirit of a Tree

Step One: Go find a strong and healthy, fairly good-sized tree. Try your own backyard or go to a neighborhood park on a nice sunny day.

Step Two: Take a walk around the tree and get a good look at it. What do you notice about the tree? Are there any animals living in it? Can you identify what variety of tree it is?

Step Three: Place the palms of your hands on the trunk of the tree, close your eyes for a moment, and ground and center. Now, tune your senses into the tree. (If you are trying to be discreet or are worried that someone will see you, try leaning your back against the trunk of the tree and then rest the palms of your hands against the trunk. If anybody walks by, you just look like you're hanging out and resting for a moment.)

Step Four: What do you feel? Sometimes it's a comprehension of a heartbeat or breathing. Either one of those sensations would make sense, as the tree is alive, after all. Trees are usually more than willing to lend a little energy to an open-minded human. If the tree exudes vibrant, healthy energy, then soak a little up.

If for some reason the tree feels funny or strange, then the tree may be sick. If this happens, you have two choices. Either thank the tree for its time and try to imagine that you are sending it a boost of healing energy. (Imagine a bright blue light coming from you and into the tree.) Or you may wish the tree well and try talking to a different tree instead.

If you imagine an intelligence coming from the tree or if you sense a definite personality, then you have more than likely just met a tree spirit. Usually friendly and good natured, tree spirits are nothing to fear. Silently ask them what they have to teach you. Let your mind drift for a moment and see what they have to say.

Step Five: Take a deep breath, slowly blow it out, and let go of the tree. Now, thank the tree for its time and leave a small token at its base—a small crystal or even a single strand of your hair will do nicely. Or you could really help out by looking around you and picking up any trash in the immediate vicinity of your new tree friend. Any of these gifts would be an acceptable way to reciprocate to the tree. Wasn't that fun?

Love Those Leaves

Check this list out. I think you will find some of the foliage from these trees will be available to you. This information is adapted for my own style of backyard magick and is based upon the traditional language of flowers.

THE FOLIAGE OF TREES AND
THEIR MAGICKAL MESSAGES

Mountain Ash (the Rowan): Brings wisdom and magick. The rowan is a Witch tree.

Elm: In floral languages, the elm stands for dignity. The elm is protective and is reported to be a popular tree with elves.

Hawthorn: This tree symbolizes hope. Part of the faerie trinity of trees, work with hawthorn blooms and foliage for love and protection and to acquire the blessings of the faeries.

Holly: In the language of flowers, the holly says "foresight" (this is another word for clairvoyance). The holly also brings about healing and protection. An old folk name for the holly is "bat wings."

Juniper: This tree and its needles encourage protection and prosperity. In the language of flowers, the juniper announces "welcome home."

Oak: The king of the trees. The oak tree is a God symbol, and in floral language its message is hospitality. The white oak stands for a free spirit, and the oak leaves represent bravery and achievement. Acorns, the fruit of the oak, are little magickal talismans that may be used to promote love, fertility, and protection.

Orange: This tropical tree represents generosity. The orange blossom was a typical bridal flower for many years as it exemplified chastity. The dried peels from its fruit are used as lucky prosperity charms.

Pear: In some floral languages, this tree speaks of justice, health, and hope. The Bradford pear tree is the number-one-selling nursery tree in the country. Even though this tree does not usually bear edible fruit, a small blooming twig would be an excellent accessory to the Protection and Balance Spell that is listed in chapter 3.

Pine: The many varieties of the pine invoke "a warm friendship." The magickal qualities of this tree were listed at the beginning of this chapter. Do you remember what they were?

Plum: In the language of flowers, the plum tree expresses integrity and honesty.

Sycamore: The sycamore tree encourages curiosity. Work with these leaves when you want to find the truth in any matter.

Willow: The weeping willow cries of a lost love. The willow is often happiest growing along the water's edge. It is a tree of Goddess and moon magick.

Creating Your Own
Foliage and Floral Spells

The various flowers and the many types of foliage from trees are supplies for practical, natural Witches. The preceding flower and foliage correspondence charts were not listed in this chapter simply to fill up the pages. All of this information is for you to benefit from. So, how do you use these various flowers and leaves in your own personal spellwork? Sit tight, and I'll show you.

Here is a spell worksheet for you to refer to. Yes, a worksheet. I told you that Witchcraft and natural magick required work, remember? When I first began to write spells and charms of my own, it really helped me to draft it all out on paper. Try using this as a reference sheet and have fun. Any Witch worth their broom writes a few of their own spells. Don't stress out, now, this is the fun stuff. This is the part of your training where you get to be creative and crafty. After all, you know what your preferences and needs are, better than anybody else.

To start this process, match up your magickal need with the coordinating natural item. Let's say that you want to design a personal spell for prosperity. So you would locate the leaf or flowers that are complementary to what you are working for, such as jasmine flowers, honeysuckle, and pine needles. Then, you would match up your harmonious candle color (in this case, green) and set the foliage around the coordinating candle. If you wanted to, you could add an aventurine stone to help draw money. After you have gathered your ingredients, try your hand at composing a simple charm. It doesn't always have to rhyme. It's time to get busy, my teenage Witch friend!

Flower and Foliage Spell Worksheet

Goal: _____

_____

_____

_____

Timing: _____

_____

Foliage or flower used: _____

_____

_____

The magickal significance of the plant: _____

_____

_____

Candle color (if you add candle magick): _____

_____

Crystals or stones: _____

_____

Charm or verse: _____

_____

_____

_____

_____

_____

Flora and the Green Man

Did you know that we have a God and Goddess specifically designated to the trees, nature, the flowers, and the garden? Yes, we do. They are the archetype of the Green Man, and the Roman goddess Flora.

The Roman goddess Flora was the queen of flowers. Most Victorian floral languages are often referred to as "Flora's Language of Flowers." This is Flora's own special way of communicating with us. Her symbols are garlands of flowers, and her sacred flower is the lupine. In ancient Rome, her lusty festival days ran from April 28 to May 3. In mythology, Flora was courted by the god Bacchus, and it is thought that she was married to the South Wind, Zephyr. This goddess was the epitome of the blossoming of all of nature. Flora is the goddess of spring and new beginnings. Wherever Flora walks, flowers are thought to bloom in her wake. The goddess Flora blesses the land with color, life, fertility, and abundance.

The Green Man has become a popular icon and garden image in the past few years. A Green Man is usually a male face surrounded by or made up of foliage, vines, and leaves. Sometimes these faces are hideous and sometimes they are amusing and charming. In truth, the Green Man is a deity that wears many masks. In modern times, the Green Man's image is used as a protector of the garden and the guardian of the wild places in nature.

The Green Man has been known throughout time as a spirit of nature and of the woods. Sometimes he was called Lord of the Green, Jack-in-the-Green, or King of the Woods.

The energy of this god is in all things, and his earthy wisdom and knowledge surround us at all times. The Green Man represents the life force of nature.

What lessons do you suppose the goddess Flora and the Green Man have been waiting to teach you? If I would have to pick just one, I believe that it would be this. Nature is sacred. The God and the Goddess may silently reveal themselves to you in many different ways. The most obvious times will be in the wild. Go outside and interact with the flowers and the trees. Pay attention to the floral messages from our

Lady Flora, and connect to nature and listen deeply to the wisdom of the Green Man. This is how you become one of the Wise Ones.

For magick is truly to be found growing all around you.

EIGHT

The God, the Goddess, and the Magickal Year

Over the years, one of the most common questions people ask me when they find out that I am a Witch is this one: "Do you believe in God?" At first, this question made me roll my eyes and sigh in exasperation. I would answer in a somewhat defensive tone, "Yes, I believe in God, and in a Goddess as well." After I had a few years of experience under my belt, I began to answer people with more care and a lot less attitude. This question is a really important one and deserves a good answer.

While my standard answer has remained basically the same, my tone has changed completely. I try to be patient and more sympathetic with my answer. "Yes, I believe in God. I also believe in the Goddess."

"Oh," is the usual response, followed by silence, as the questioner stands there and thinks about it for a moment. And just like my conversation that I had with one of my teenage nephews recently, some of the more common follow-up questions are, "Who is the Goddess? Is she equal to the God? Where does the Goddess come from . . . what does she look like . . . what is her name?"

The answer is that she has many names and many faces, as does her consort and other equal half, the God. From all over the world and from many cultures, during ancient times to the present day, the God and the Goddess are known and worshiped. Some of the titles that people have called them by and their stories may seem somewhat familiar to you.

They are the Earth Mother and the Sky Father to the indigenous people of the Americas. To the ancient Egyptians, they were the married partnership of Isis and Osiris. Isis was worshiped for over three thousand years. She was not only popular in Egypt, but throughout Greece and into Europe as well. Isis was known as the Queen of Heaven and the Lady of Life. She was usually depicted as holding her son on her lap, as is her modern counterpart of today, the Virgin Mary.

In the ancient mystical tradition of Judaism, the God and Goddess were known as Yahweh and the Shekinah. The Shekinah is called both Beloved and Bride, and is thought to be the source of wisdom and spirit. She is a companion and a guide to those who seek her out. Together, this God and Goddess help people connect their spiritual life to their everyday lives.

To the Sumerians, the Goddess was called Inanna. She was venerated by many titles, including Queen of Heaven and Earth, Light of the World, and Lady of all Powers. Inanna was a fertility goddess, and her lover/consort's name was Tammuz.

From the Ireland of olden times there was the father god called Dagda (known as the "Good God") and a mother goddess called Danu. Danu was the mother of the race called the Tuatha de Danann, meaning "the children of Danu."

There is also the triple goddess Brigid. Variations on her name include Brigit, Bride, Brighid, and Brigantia. No matter how hard the ruling church tried, they could not get the ancient people to give up their favored local goddess. So, finally, the church gave in and "transformed" her into a saint. Brigid then became a favored saint of the Celts. She was worshiped at an abbey in Kildare, Ireland, where a fire was kept burning continuously in her honor. All over Ireland and Britain there are places known as Brigid's wells. These are springs and wells dedicated to the goddess Brigid. She was and is still revered in Ireland, Scotland, Britain, and France. Brigid is a very popular figure with the modern Witches of today as a goddess of fire, poetry, and inspiration.

In America, we have a couple of local goddesses that you may already be familiar with. There is the fire and volcano goddess Pele from Hawaii, and the Lady of Guadalupe from south of the border in Mexico. The Lady of Guadalupe, sometimes referred to as the Queen of the Americas, is a Mother Goddess figure. She is celebrated and honored by many cultures, both magickal and mundane, throughout North and South America.

Lastly, here is another good example of a god story, and one that will stretch your comprehension of religion. Take a look at the Persian god of light and compassion known as Mithras. The sun god Mithras is an extremely interesting mythological character. He was born in a cave of a virgin mother (some mythologies claim that he was born from a rock or in a cave—sort of self-generated), and attended by shepherds and three wise men at his birth. His birthday was celebrated on December 25.

Mithras was known as the light of the world, son of righteousness, and the Savior. He had twelve followers or disciples, and his resurrection was celebrated at the spring equinox. (Boy, does he remind you of anyone?) He taught love and understanding to his followers all at about two thousand years before the creation of Christianity. Are you sensing a variation on a theme here? You bet you are.

Now that I've got you to thinking, let's get into the mythologies and ideas of the God and the Goddess. Let's discuss how they work together and relate to natural magick and to the magickal year.

The Triple Goddess

The Goddess of Witchcraft is seen as a triple goddess. She has three faces, or sides, to her personality: the maiden, the mother, and the crone. Each face of the Goddess matches up to a different specialty in magick and to a particular phase of the moon. Those three main moon phases are waxing, full, and waning: waxing moon for the maiden, full moon for the mother, and the waning or dark of the moon for the crone.

The maiden is a young girl, sometimes called the virgin. The term *virgin* refers to the fact that she is whole, complete unto herself. She belongs to no one. She is the huntress. She is wise and she will help us to "hunt down" the right path to follow in life. She represents the season of spring, fun, laughter, freedom, excitement, and new beginnings. The maiden helps us embrace the fun and excitement of living. Her names include Artemis, Athena, Bast, Brigit, Diana, Elaine, Eostre, Kore, Minerva, Parvati, and Persephone. The maiden's color is white—for initiation, freshness, and purity.

The mother represents the season of summer and harvest. She may be pictured as being pregnant or with her children. She is strong, mature, and powerful in her own right. The mother is the generous teacher. Her love for her children never fades. Her magickal associations are birth, love, marriage, fertility, prosperity, stability, and healing. The mother's sacred color is red, to symbolize the color of blood and birth. Her names include Aphrodite, Ceres, Demeter, Freya, Hera, Inanna, Isis, Kwan Yin, Lady of Guadalupe, Mary, Selene, Tara, and Yemaya.

The crone represents the season of winter. She is seen as the old wisewoman and the third face of the Goddess. She is the wise, loving old grandmother who comforts, and the frightening crone in the black cape, stirring her cauldron of renewal, all at once. The crone is often the most difficult of the faces of the Goddess to understand, simply because she is a contradiction.

The crone stands for judgment, death, and rebirth. The lessons that we learn from the crone are love, acceptance, and patience. The crone's sacred color is black—not the color of death, but the color of deep space and possibilities. Her names include Cailleach, Cerridwen, Hecate, Holda, Kali, Lilith, the Morrigan, Morgan le Fay, Nephthys, and Tiamat.

A Triple Goddess Ritual

Here is a little get-acquainted ritual for you. You may use this as an introduction to a meditation or just to introduce yourself to the Triple Goddess and to ask for her guidance and blessing. You will be working with the four elements in this ritual and invoking (calling upon) the three aspects of the Goddess.

Supplies needed:

- Seashells (one or two is plenty)

- A moonstone (tumbling stones are perfect)

- A cup or goblet to hold water

- A white flower in a vase (a rose or lily is lovely, or you can go with whatever kind of white flower is in season or available). Don't forget to check out your yard. A white geranium, daisy, or petunia bloom is perfectly acceptable.

- A white votive candle and a holder

- A nail or needle, to scratch a triple moon symbol on the side of the candle

- Matches or a lighter

- A safe, flat work surface to set up on

Perform on the night of a full moon. (Check the calendar or almanac.) You may work at moon rise, when the moon is entirely visible in the eastern sky. Or you can wait until the moon is up and directly overhead. Carve the triple moon symbol carefully onto the side of the votive. Votive candles are soft, so you will not have to apply a lot of pressure to scratch the symbol on the side. Place the candle in the holder. Arrange the moonstone and shells around the votive holder. Set the vase containing your white flower off to the side, away from the heat of the candle flame. Put the cup holding the water on the opposite side of the candle. Light the candle and say,

> *Blessed be the Dark Crone, the Bright Mother, and the Youthful Maiden,*
>
> *I request your blessing and guidance, I am one of your children.*
>
> *By the powers of fire and water, I call for courage and love,*
>
> *the powers of earth and air, bring me strength and wisdom from above.*

If you care to try a meditation on one of the many faces of the Goddess, this would be the time and place to do so. Close your eyes, get comfortable, and relax. Imagine that you are walking quietly in a moonlit garden. It is a soft, warm night; a full moon sails overhead and illuminates the path. You amble along, heading nowhere in particular. An arbor covered in blooms catches your eye—it appears to be a gateway into another hidden part of the garden. Tall shrubs flank either side of the arbor, blocking off your view. It is the entrance to a secret garden.

You decide to investigate. As you walk closer to the hedge and the arbor, you realize that the pale blooms are roses. They are luminous and bright white. You breathe in the scent and decide to see what is on the other side of the secret garden. As you duck under the arbor that is heavy with blooms, a few fragrant petals sprinkle down and land softly into your hair. As you pass through the arbor, you see in the garden a simple stone bench, where a woman sits, illuminated in the moonlight.

She turns to look at you. She is radiantly beautiful and draped in a flowing white gown. Her long hair is silvery blonde and it ripples down her back. On her brow, a silver crescent moon catches the light and gleams softly. As you stand there for a moment, transfixed at the sight of the Moon Goddess, a white owl swoops past you and lights in an apple tree above the Lady.

The Lady smiles and beckons you to her. You join her on the bench and she holds out a hand for you. You smile, take her hand, and look into her calm, grey eyes. A sense of peace and great love settles over you. "I've been expecting you," she tells you gently. Listen to what lessons she has to teach you. When you are finished with your meditation, thank the Lady for her time and attention. Leave the secret garden by passing back through the rose arbor.

Close the ritual by saying,

Thank you, Goddess, for your love and care.
I close this ritual now by the powers of earth, water, fire, and air.

Allow the candle to burn itself out. You may need to move it to a safer location if you are outdoors. If you have to move the candle inside, rearrange the shells and the moonstone when you go back in. Ground and center when you are finished.

The God: The Earth Father

The God in the religion of Wicca has many names and many faces. The God is seen as the divine child, a handsome young man, and then a wise, mature king who lays down his life so his people may live. His story directly revolves in harmony with the cycles of the four seasons of the year.

Now, before someone gets in a huff, let's set one thing straight. From time to time, you may see the God referred to as the Horned God. Relax, don't get excited now, we are not speaking of the Christian bad guy. The Horned God has the antlers of a stag—you know, a male deer. The stag is a representation of the old agricultural gods of ancient people. The ancient people were hunters and gatherers; they hunted to survive. You had better believe that they were thankful to the animals who gave up their lives so they could then feed their families. The animals were never killed for sport, and none of the animal was wasted. They used the hides for many things, including clothing, and the bones were carved into tools. The fact that ancient people used the symbolism of a stag as a portrayal of the male aspect of the God is really no big surprise, then. Feel better now? Good.

A God Ritual

Here is another ritual using natural supplies. This one will help you get to know and be comfortable with the many faces of the God of Nature. If you are facing a challenge of some kind, whether it is a sport that you participate in or a more personal challenge, try calling on the God for a little extra strength and stamina. In this outdoor ritual, you are calling on the Green Man. The Green Man is a familiar Pagan icon. Found today at most garden accessory stores, this popular and benevolent image of the God is fun and friendly. Traditionally the Green Man is portrayed as a man's smiling face made up of leaves and foliage.

Supplies needed:

- A handful of oak leaves, a few acorns, or pine cones

- A tiger's-eye tumbling stone

- A green votive candle (pine or herb scented would be good)

- A votive holder

- A nail or needle to carve the sun symbol onto the sides of the candle

- Lighter or matches

- A safe, flat work surface to set your supplies on

Work this ritual at noon or at sunrise. Call on the God for strength and stamina. Call on the Green Man to bring both protection and laughter into your life. Arrange the stone, the leaves, and acorns or pine cones around the candleholder in a loose circle. Light the candle. If you would like to try a meditation on the God, do so after the charm is spoken.

The noble Green Man is but one face of the God of olden times,

see his face in the oak leaves and in the rising sun that shines.

Acorns and pine cones are his symbols, sacred they may be,

bring laughter and compassion into my days, grant me a victory.

For your meditation, imagine that you are in a forest during high summer. As you make your way deeper into the woods, you become aware that you have entered into a natural circle of oak trees. The forest becomes hushed and you realize that you have just entered a sacred place. You begin to feel a little disoriented and the woods feel close and humid. You shake your head to get rid of the feeling.

Within the circle of the trees tumbles a cold and clear stream. That should help, you decide. You walk into the center of the circle and kneel down alongside the stream. You cup your hands into the clear stream and splash some water onto your face and neck to help you cool off. As you raise your head, feeling refreshed, you notice a tall, bearded man standing across the stream from you.

He is accompanied by many forest creatures. A stag, a doe, and a spotted fawn stand calmly by his side. You are not alarmed at his unexpected appearance, for you know, deep in your heart, who this must be. He is dressed in a robe of dark green and there are holly and oak leaves twined in his curling brown hair. A tawny owl stands as a sentinel in an oak branch above him. Brown rabbits sit, with their noses twitching, next to his bare feet. He stays where he is and spreads out his hands in a peaceful gesture of greeting.

"You are welcome here," he announces.

You smile and thank him. He asks you to sit and be comfortable. You sit easily down on your side of the stream. As he sits down cross- legged on his side, all of the accompanying animals, except the fawn, settle in as well. The fawn picks its way nimbly across the little stream and eases its way close to you. You sit still as it leans in carefully and sniffs at your hair. A small laugh escapes you. The fawn springs back and then, with a joyous leap, it jumps and bounds playfully back to its mother's side. It curls itself up next to the doe and she nudges it playfully as it nestles in. The God is smiling approvingly at you. You take a moment to ground and center yourself, and then you listen to what he has to say . . .

When you are finished with your meditation, thank the God for his time and attention. Then leave the sacred circle of oak trees the way that you came.

Close the ritual by saying,

I thank the God for his time and care.

I close this ritual now by the powers of earth, water, fire, and air.

Allow the candle to burn out. If you need to move the candle inside to finish burning safely, do so. Remember to ground and center when you are finished.

Want to learn more? The God and the Goddess are out there, waiting for you to start your own personal voyage of discovery. Take this opportunity and study different mythologies and different cultures. Try starting with the Greek/Roman pantheon—everybody has to study those in high school. Move on to the Norse, the Egyptian, and the Celtic deities. Look into the Hindu, African, Native American, and Asian cultures as well. You will probably have a few favorite deities right away. That's fine, just keep your mind open to other possibilities. Now use this time to study and decide for yourself who you like and who you are the most comfortable with. Pay attention and see who presents themselves to you. Nothing happens by accident. Learn their stories and see where this path leads you.

The Wheel of the Year

Witches follow a solar calendar of eight holidays, or sabbats. The sabbats are celebrated in harmony with changing seasons and the old Celtic agricultural holidays. As Witches, we follow and celebrate the changing seasons of the earth, and delight in the cycles of the sun, moon, and the stars. The wheel of the year and the eight sabbats that Witches observe celebrate the story of the God and Goddess. The God is connected to the Goddess in the Wiccan religion and their story is a cyclical one.

He is the sacred child born to a divine mother at the winter solstice. The winter solstice is the time of the longest night and the shortest day. From this point on, however, the days grow longer and the light grows stronger. In the weeks that follow, during the bleakest part of winter, the sun begins to gain strength and the God grows to a boy. At the halfway point of winter and spring, we celebrate Imbolc, also called Candlemas. It is a festival of light.

The God is pictured as a young man who falls in love with the maiden Goddess at the spring equinox. As all of nature rejoices in new beginnings and growth, so do we. Colored eggs, white rabbits, and flowers all feature prominently in our celebrations. The white rabbit is a symbol for the Goddess and of fertility. Colored eggs are traditionally a symbol of new life. (You may find it interesting to note that the Druids of olden times exchanged red-dyed eggs with each other as a symbol of life and in celebration of the Earth renewing itself.)

The marriage of the God and Goddess is celebrated at the cross-quarter day, or halfway point of spring and summer, on May Day—*Beltane*, as Witches call it. The garden is in high gear and the flowers are starting to bloom as the daylight hours grow longer and longer. Maypoles and baskets of flowers are traditional symbols for this holiday.

The God and Goddess then join together at midsummer and conceive a child. This is the height of the Sun King's glory and his power. Astrologically, the sun at the summer solstice is at its highest point in the sky. The garden and the flowers are in full bloom, and it seems as though summer could last forever. However, from this point of year on, the sun loses its strength and the days begin to shorten. (Symbolically, as the sun's potency fades, the God grows older.)

The cross-quarter day, or halfway point, of summer and autumn falls on August 1, the sabbat of Lammas. At this time, the God is the wise king and ruler of his people. This is the first harvest of grains and berries. As September arrives, the God is the mature God of the second harvest. Apples and pumpkins are harvested and the grain crops are cut down, as is the stag, who gives his life for his people so they can survive. The God dies at the sabbat of Mabon, the autumnal equinox. This is not a sad time, however; take a look at the glory of the changing leaves around you. This is the Witches' Thanksgiving, a time of plenty and harvest.

The God returns to the underworld and rests during Samhain, otherwise known as Halloween. Another cross-quarter day and the half point of autumn and winter, this is a dark time of year as the leaves are faded and falling from the trees. The crone Goddess rules at this time of year. All of the crops are now gathered in. The weather begins to turn colder, as all of nature rests with the God as he awaits his time to be reborn. Then, at the winter solstice—Yule—when the sun begins to strengthen, he will be reborn to the Goddess once more.

Their story coordinates with the annual season cycle, and so it repeats itself every year. Our calendar is both a circular and a seasonal one. Each one of the eight sabbats or holidays makes up one of the eight spokes on the year's wheel. This is why the Witches' calendar is called the wheel of the year.

The Witches' Holidays:
The Eight Sabbats

Each sabbat indicates an important moment of change in the earth and her seasons. At the winter solstice, the sun is at its lowest point in the sky. From this point on, the daylight hours will slowly increase and the sun will rise a little earlier each morning. At the equinoxes, day and night hours are of equal balance. At the summer solstice, the sun reaches its highest point in the sky and the daylight hours begin to slowly decrease. This is noticeable as the sun will begin to set a little earlier each evening.

The eight sabbats are divided up into two categories: the lesser sabbats and the greater sabbats. Here is a tip to help you remember which holiday belongs to which category. The four lesser sabbats have calendar dates that change from year to year, because they are celebrated on the day of the astrological event of the annual solstices and equinoxes, usually between the twentieth and the twenty-third of their respective months. The calendar date never remains the same from year to year because they are celebrated in harmony with the solar cycles and in tune with the sun as it enters a certain astrological sign. This would be a good time to check and make sure what day they fall on this year. Write your answer down in a notebook. Entitle these pages "The Sabbats."

If you are unsure of how to find out when these solstice and equinox dates occur during the year, try checking an ordinary calendar. It's actually very easy to tell when the dates for the solstice and equinox are. Look for the first day of winter, spring, summer, and fall. Those are the four lesser sabbats. You can always refer to the Farmer's Almanac or another astrological guide, like *Llewellyn's Magical Almanac*, for the exact date and time of the seasonal equinoxes and solstices.

The Lesser Sabbats:
The Equinoxes and the Solstices

Yule

Yule, also called Midwinter, or simply winter solstice. This holiday occurs in the month of December on the first day of winter, the day of the winter solstice. Evergreens and pine have traditionally been used to decorate the home since olden times. Bringing greenery into your home for the winter holidays was not a Christian invention, it was a Pagan one. This act gave the people hope that spring would indeed return to the land.

Natural decorations and symbols include a sparkling tree covered in ornaments and decorated wreaths. The wreath is thought to be an archaic symbol of the wheel of the year. Pine boughs are utilized to drape over doorways and across fireplace mantels. Don't forget to deck the halls with holly and hang up some nice Druidic mistletoe. (For safety's sake, keep mistletoe well out of reach of young siblings—it's poisonous if ingested.)

More decorations for this Witches' winter holiday include the Yule log. The Yule log is a centerpiece made out of a half of a decorative log. This log is studded with three red candles and adorned with holly, ivy, and pine. The Yule log may also be a fireplace log trimmed with holly and evergreen that has been attached with a festive ribbon. During the winter solstice festivities, the embellished log is ritually burned in the fireplace (or the candles are lit if the Yule log is a centerpiece) to bring good luck and prosperity to the family. Colors for the holiday include gold, for the newly born sun; white, for the winter ice and snows; deep green, to symbolize the evergreen and prosperity; and, finally, red, the color of winter holly berries and the Mother Goddess.

Ostara

Ostara, pronounced *O-star-ah*, is celebrated in March, on the first day of spring, the day of the vernal (spring) equinox. This is the festival of the Norse goddess of spring, Eostre. Her sacred natural symbols are spring flowers, to represent nature renewing herself; the white rabbit, for fertility; and colored eggs, to symbolize rebirth. Now, you can stop wondering where the Easter Bunny came from—he is actually Eostre's sacred rabbit of fertility. A pretty way to decorate for this holiday would be to set out a few pots of blooming daffodils or tulips in your house. Don't forget to dye some eggs with your family. If you want to, decorate the eggs in a witchy fashion, with moons and suns and stars. Colors for this sabbat include all pastel colors: sky blue, sunny yellow, pink, lavender, and spring green.

Midsummer

Also called Litha, pronounced *lee-tha*, or simply the summer solstice. This sabbat occurs in the month of June on the first day of summer, the date of the summer solstice. The summer solstice is a time for faeries, the Green Man, and flower magick. If you live near the water, go swimming and collect some shells or stones. Lay out on the beach, the shore, or even at the pool, and feel the strength of the sun as the rays shine down on you. (Don't forget to wear sunscreen. We don't want you to get burned.) The sun is at its highest point in the sky today, so go and celebrate it!

Natural symbols for this day include herbs, roses, and flowers in all shades from the garden. Don't forget the seashells. Some Witches really get into the whole Midsummer-water-ocean thing and use a magickal mermaid theme. They decorate with ropes of pearl-looking beads, starfish, and seashells. Go with whatever theme you like the best.

Traditional Witches' colors for this festival are gold, green, and red. I like to put a modern spin on this holiday and use shades of blue and metallic gold instead. Celestial stickers, confetti, plates, and party supplies are easy to come by and fun to use for your celebration. Try reading Shakespeare's *A Midsummer Night's Dream*. Wait up in the garden tonight and get in the mood to meet the faeries!

Mabon

Mabon, pronounced *May-bon*, is the autumnal equinox. This sabbat is celebrated in the month of September, on the first day of fall. It is the second harvest festival and the Witches' Thanksgiving. Traditional decorations include apples, fall leaves, Indian corn, grapes, pumpkins, and the overflowing cornucopia. At my house, this day means a turkey dinner with all the trimmings, including pumpkin pie. A simple way to celebrate this festival is to do what my family does. We go apple picking. If you can't manage to do that, pick up some fresh apples or grapes from a fruit stand or farmer's market and make yourself a picnic lunch. It's the perfect excuse to check out if the leaves are starting to turn in your neck of the woods. Colors for this holiday include autumn shades and tones of brown, gold, red, orange, and yellow.

The Greater Sabbats:
The Fire Festivals

The four greater sabbats are sometimes referred to as fire festivals. Tradition has it that on these days great bonfires were lit by the ancient people as a celebration of the wheel of the year turning. In some parts of Great Britain and here in the U. S., these traditional bonfires are still being burned. These four greater sabbats fall on cross-quarter days, which are the halfway points between the seasons.

Candlemas

Candlemas or Imbolc (pronounced *Em-bolg*) is a festival of light. This cross-quarter day is celebrated on February 2. Here in the United States, it is also known as Groundhog Day. The midpoint of winter and spring, for Witches it is the day to celebrate the Goddess as a maiden. Candle and fire magick are traditional. In the Celtic tradition, this is also the festival day of the goddess Brigid. As stated earlier, this beloved Celtic goddess is a triple goddess of fire, poetry, and inspiration. Colors for Imbolc / Candlemas include white to symbolize the snow, and purple for the crocuses that are starting to break through the frozen ground. At this time of year, a fun decoration is pots of fragrant, purple hyacinths that florists are selling for Valentine's Day. I picked up a pot of hyacinths at a local home improvement store for under five dollars. Purple and white African violets are another nice and inexpensive way to add flowers to your sabbat ritual.

It will come as no surprise that candles feature prominently in this sabbat. This past Imbolc / Candlemas, my circle performed an uncomplicated ritual to celebrate Brigid's day and to welcome the early spring. My daughter, Kat, came into the circle as the maiden Brigid. As she entered the circle, she had her head down and was completely covered in a long, black, hooded cape. She was carrying in her hands a large iron cauldron that contained a single lit candle inside of a holder. Around the burning candle were several ribbon-wrapped votive candles, one candle for each person who was in the circle that night. As the circle was ritually closed behind her, she tossed her hood back to reveal a maiden's wreath of daisies that she was wearing in her long hair.

"I am the goddess Brigid," she announced to the group, as she placed the cauldron down and into the center of the circle.

"Brigid is come! Brigid is welcome!" the group replied. After Kat took her place in the circle, I handed out challenges to each member of the group. Each challenge was written on a piece of parchment paper and tied with a silk crocus bud and a lavender-colored ribbon. Each tiny scroll held a magickal symbol and a single individual challenge word that each person was to meditate on. They were to share what they had learned with their sisters the next time we got together, at the sabbat of Ostara.

After a guided meditation, we gave out tealights to each member of the group. I lit my tealight first from the cauldron fire, as I made a request to Brigid for the coming year. My daughter touched her candle to mine and made her silent request. Kat then touched her candle flame to her neighbor's, and around the circle it went, in a clockwise direction, until everyone held a piece of Brigid's fire.

The burning candles were then passed around to the person standing nearest the altar, where they were lined up in front of a framed picture of Brigid. These candles represented our hopes and dreams for the coming year. It was nice to see them all lined up and watched over by Brigid. We allowed the little tealights to burn merrily away until they went out on their own later that evening. The remaining ribbon-tied votive candles in the cauldron were blessed and given out for the circle members to take home, to use however they saw fit.

Beltane

Beltane begins its observance on Beltane Eve at sundown on April 31. Beltane Day is celebrated on May 1, otherwise known as May Day. This is the midpoint of spring and summer, the time when we celebrate the marriage of the God and the Goddess. Maypoles and baskets of spring flowers are traditional decorations. Colors can range from the traditional red and white to bridesmaid colors of purple, hot pink, yellow, and bright green and blue. Natural decorations are flowers, handheld bouquets of flowers, and more flowers tucked in jars full of water or arranged in May baskets and hung on doors.

Beltane is a fun and rowdy sabbat. It is a time to play, sing, dance, and make music. This is one of the times of the year when the veil between out world and the Faerie realm is at its most thin (the other being Samhain). Try making some simple sugar cookies and leaving a circle of the crumbs out for the faeries and the animals.

You could go on a nature walk in the park or drag a blanket out into the backyard. Get outside and enjoy the outdoors! Settle down in nature somewhere and try a little meditation to see if you can communicate with the nature spirits and the faeries. Don't fall asleep! If you do, legend says you may be kidnapped into the Faerie realm. All teasing aside, I'd love to see you try to explain that to your mother as the reason you came home late for dinner.

Lammas

Lammas (pronounced *lah-mas*) or Lughnasadh (pronounced *loo-na-sa*) is observed on August 1. This is the midpoint of summer and fall, the harvest of berries and grains, and the first of three harvest festivals. This sabbat is celebrated with herb gathering and bread baking. Natural decorations include sunflowers, marigolds, gourds, and dried wheat. Candle colors for this sabbat include green, golden yellow, orange, and soft shades of red.

At the first of the three harvest festivals, be thankful for the things that you do have and for your right to be free. Go berry picking. Go on a nature walk with your family. You can always meet your buddies up at the public pool and go swimming. Hey, it's hot outside! Cool off and help out the plants and trees in your yard at the same time by watering them. You can always use this as the perfect opportunity to playfully nail one of your family members with a hose.

For some reason, my teenage kids and their friends seem to dance carefully around me whenever I am watering the garden. They never turn their backs on me. I suppose they are a bit nervous of being around me when I have a hose in my hand. Why? Because they know I may squirt them down at any given time. (Keeps them on their toes.)

Don't even roll your eyes at me. When was the last time you played in the sprinkler or had a water fight? It is fun to play outside. Yes, I realize that you are a cool teenager and you have an image to uphold. Now go and have some fun, will ya? Laugh and enjoy yourself! I am often at my happiest and most content when I'm digging around in the garden. (Maybe it's because I like to play in the dirt.) How about you? What simple things make you happy?

Are you noticing that the days are definitely growing shorter? The wheel of the year is turning. Summer is quickly drawing to a close, so you better enjoy your summer vacation while you still have it!

Samhain

Samhain (pronounced *sow-en*) is a cross-quarter day and the one most associated with Witches and magick. Samhain is celebrated on the evening of October 31. It is the final harvest festival and the Celtic New Year. This is the midpoint of autumn and winter. At this time of year, the doorway or portals between our world and the spirit world are very thin. The crone is reigning at this time of the year, and you see her likeness in the Halloween type of old, scary Witch that is everywhere. The traditional colors for this sabbat are, of course, black and orange. Natural symbols are autumn leaves, ornamental corn, pumpkins, gourds, and jack-o'-lanterns.

So how does a real Witch and her family celebrate Halloween/Samhain? Well, this Witch lavishly decorates the house both inside and out. In the front yard, we set up a scarecrow, several bundles of cornstalks, and display many of the pumpkins that we grew at our family farm. That evening we put out a buffet of our favorite party foods, and my teenagers hang out and help me pass out candy to the little ones. I pass out both candy and the miniature pumpkins that we grew at the farm to the neighborhood trick-or-treaters. Our youngest nieces and many young nephews drop by to show us their costumes and then, later in the evening, my family settles in and we all watch a movie together. (Pretty scary, huh?)

After everyone else heads off to bed for the night, I usually perform a quiet solitary ritual to honor any loved ones who have passed, such as my grandparents.

I don't care what you may have been told, but Halloween, or Samhain, as Witches call it, is not a night for violence and horror. For Witches, this holiday is the beginning of the winter season. Samhain is a time to remember your loved ones who have passed away, and a time to celebrate the final harvest and to be thankful for your blessings.

A Teen Samhain Ritual

If you'd like to try a simple Samhain ritual, gather together these things.

- A black and an orange candle (these are illuminator candles)

- One yard of black fabric, or a dark scarf

- A small carved pumpkin with a candle (any color) burning inside of it (use one of your jack-o'-lanterns from Halloween)

- A dove feather (use a fallen feather only!). Do not take a feather from a live bird. If you cannot locate a dove's feather, then use a plain white or grey feather. Hint: You can purchase these feathers at tackle shops, where they sell fly-tying supplies, or at an arts and crafts store.

- Photos or pictures of any loved ones and/or pets that have passed away (these should be individuals who loved you very much)

Set up your supplies on a small table or tray. If possible, cover the table with a dark scarf or fabric of some kind. Light up the pumpkin's candle and arrange the orange and black candles on either side. Spread out the photos that you have of your loved ones in front of the jack-o'-lantern. Light the orange and black candles. Ground and center. Speak this invocation.

With these enchanted candles and by their light,

I remember these beloved spirits this Samhain night.

I have not forgotten you, you are still much loved

I send you my greetings on the wings of a dove.

Watch over and protect me, I ask this of you.

Help me to be brave and wise in all that I do.

Close the ritual by saying,

The portal between the worlds is now closed.

By all the powers of three times three, as I will it, so shall it be.

The added line about "closing the portals" is simply a precautionary one. No, you did not open anything, but if this ritual is performed on Samhain night, the veil between the worlds is very thin. By saying this line you reinforce that nothing—like a ghost—can come across and into your world. Samhain/Halloween is a very magickal time; anything can and will happen. Can't you feel it in the air?

Now set the pumpkin in a safe place to allow the candle to finish burning. (Leave the lid off so it won't scorch.) Extinguish your Samhain illuminator candles and save them for next year's celebration. Leave the photos in place for a few days. Every time you see them, try to recall a good memory or something sweet or funny about the individual.

Hitting the Books

Try your hand at celebrating all of the sabbats. Discover more about the many faces of the God and Goddess and how they correlate to the wheel of the year. Keep your celebrations uncomplicated and have fun! There are many good sources for learning about the Witches' holidays. Remember to hit the library and see what you can find. Check the reading list below for some good books to read to learn more about the God and the Goddess and our magickal year.

Further Reading

On the God and Goddess:

Harvey, Andrew, and Anne Barring. *The Divine Feminine* (Conari Press, 1996).

Blair, Nancy. *Goddesses for Every Season* (Element Books, 1995).

Matthews, John. *The Quest for the Green Man* (Quest Books, 2001).

Monaghan, Patricia. *The Book of Goddesses and Heroines* (Llewellyn, 1990).

On the wheel of the year:

Cabot, Laurie, and Jean Mills. *Celebrate the Earth: A Year of Holidays in the Pagan Tradition* (Delta Books, 1994).

Campanelli, Pauline. *Ancient Ways* (Llewellyn, 1993).

Ferguson, Diana. *The Magickal Year* (Labyrinth Publishing, 1996).

NINE

Four Tools,
Four Elements

A teenage Witch stands, breathless and nervous, at the checkout counter of a local magick shop. So many nifty magickal tools and accessories to choose from! Which ones should she choose? "I really want to do this right, you know," she whispers to the friend that she dragged along.

The friend rolls her eyes and urges the shopper to hurry up. The teen chews on her bottom lip as she tries to decide. Should she purchase the expensive beeswax tapers or just go and buy little votives at the grocery store for fifty cents? Does she need an expensive holder or will a regular glass votive cup fill the purpose? They were a heck of a lot cheaper at the grocery store, she recalls.

The Teen Witch's stomach begins to churn as she eyes the pretty ceramic pentacle on display, and then asks herself how much she can really afford to buy today. "I don't have a wand, a pentacle, or even a ritual cup," she reminds herself. "I can't be a real Witch without those things. What should I do?" she wonders.

Hang on a minute. Calm down and save your money. You have lots of time to find those spiffy little tools—and a Witch is not judged by his or her wand alone. Everything that you need to practice natural magick is to be found in one of two places: yourself and the outdoors. Natural magick does not require the use of a lot of special ritual tools, because you and the elements *are* the tools. The whole point of this book is to teach you to work with simple, down-to-earth supplies and in harmony with the magick of nature.

However, I do realize that everybody likes *the stuff*: the accessories, the doodads, and the traditional tools that Witches use. When I first began to seriously practice magick, I wanted a set of Witch's tools badly, but I could not afford the ones that I saw in occult supply catalogs. However, I have a husband who likes to do woodworking, and I enjoy arts and crafts. So, I wondered, why couldn't we construct them ourselves? When our children were small, we actually used to supplement our income during the holidays by selling his woodworking and my tool painting at craft shows.

The more I thought about it, the better I liked this idea. If we made the tools ourselves, wouldn't that imbue them with more magickal energy? What if I timed the creation of the tools to finish them on the day of the full moon? *Hmm . . .*

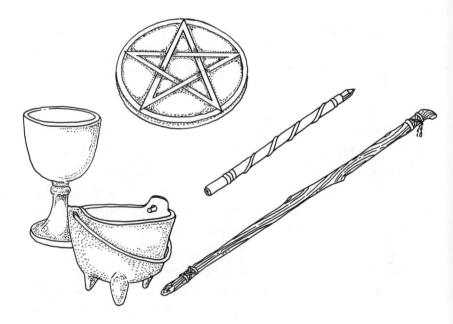

Tools of the Trade

If you recall, in each of the chapters on the elements there was a correspondence chart. In that chart was a listing of a traditional Witch's tool that harmonized with each element. (I told you that we'd be coming back to those correspondence charts.)

For the remainder of this chapter, the sections will be broken down into the four main tools that Witches often use. We will follow that up with some information on magickal work spaces, and ways to discreetly set them up. To keep things in a natural magick theme, I am going to give you some practical tips, information, and directions about how to make these tools yourself out of natural items. I will also suggest some earthy items for you to decorate your magickal work spaces with.

What kind of natural items will you be incorporating into your magickal tools? How about assorted hardwoods for your pentacles? For the construction of a wand, I suggest working with small branches from various magickal trees. You may use wood-burning tools or acrylic paints to decorate your handmade tools. Go with whatever you like. This is your chance to use your imagination and to be magickally creative and crafty. You know, it really is true what they say—Witches are crafty people.

The Wand: Air

The magick wand. It makes us imagine wise old wizards and fairy godmothers granting wishes to unfortunate girls. Every kid has imagined themselves using a magick wand when they were little. They are part and parcel of what we associate with Witches, magick, and spellcasting.

Witches use wands to help them cast their personal magickal power out toward a specific magickal goal. The wand is used to propel and direct your personal power/magickal energy—sort of like a magickal extension of your arm.

The wand is a tool of invocation. To invoke something is to call on it. In other words if you invoke the Egyptian cat goddess Bast, you are calling on her, inviting her to come to you, and asking the Goddess for her help. A good example of invoking or calling on the goddess Bast is the Come Home Kitten Spell of my daughter's from the introduction.

It still surprises me that one of the questions people ask when they get to know me is whether or not I really have a wand. The answer is . . . yes, I do. In fact, I have several. Some are dramatic, and some are homely and simple. One is made out of a dowel rod that I purchased from the hardware store, and topped with a small quartz crystal. Another wand is that gnarled and twisted piece of driftwood that I found on the shores of Lake Michigan. A few wands are fancier and made up of large crystal points, wire sculpture, and copper tubing.

My husband made those copper wands for me. I use those wands selectively because things tend to blow up, like the lightbulbs in lamps, if I wave them around too much. Well, it makes sense—copper does conduct electricity. Those copper wands now have leather-wrapped handles for insulation, so they are not as problematic.

My first wand was pretty modest—actually it was downright ugly. It was the plain dowel rod with a quartz crystal point messily hot-glued onto the end. I tried to make it look nicer by wrapping the dowel rod in purple yarn. It didn't help much. I had made the wand in secret and I was so embarrassed by the way it looked that I wouldn't even let my woodworking husband see it. At the time, I was convinced that if I did not at least own some sort of wand, then I probably wasn't even a "real" Witch after all. So, determinedly, I consecrated the wand at the first available full moon and then I stashed it away, behind my books.

The first time I went to use the wand, it was Beltane evening. I was sitting within my circle, wand in hand, when I experienced something rather unusual. Somehow the crystal point refracted and it threw rainbows of colored light all over the floor. So what's so unusual about that? Some quartz crystals can make prisms of light . . .

Well, let me explain. When this event happened, it was night, and I only had a few candles burning for illumination. There was no light source strong enough in the room to have caused the prism effect. I sat there, feeling the hair rise up on the back of my neck, and laughed softly at the wonder and magick that I held in my hands. Even though I now own prettier or more aesthetically pleasing wands, I still have and use my first plain, yarn-wrapped wand.

So don't worry so much about whether or not the wand is fancy or pretty. If you make it yourself with positive intentions and consecrate the tool correctly, it will work just fine. Now that we've gotten you to thinking, here are some basic directions for wand construction.

A good rule of thumb for choosing the correct size of wand for yourself is to measure the length of your arm, from the palm of your hand to the inside of your elbow. If you are working with a thin, fallen branch, you may choose to leave the bark on. An old, bleached-out piece of driftwood makes a great wand, especially if it's all twisted and curvy. A driftwood wand could, in fact, be used to call forth positive emotions, loving feelings, and healing energy, since it's been imbued with so much watery energy.

Take the tapered end of the stick or small branch and carefully hot-glue a quartz crystal point to the end. Then wrap some thin copper jewelry wire around the crystal and the branch tip so that the crystal is attached securely to the wood. You may decorate the thicker handle end of the wand with ribbons or silken cords of your favorite color. To embellish the wand further, tie on some small beads, charms, or a fallen feather to your handle's cords. Check out the local arts and crafts stores for jewelry wire, beads, cords, and celestial charms.

The Staff: Fire

The tool that many traditional Witches customarily associate with the element of fire is the athame (pronounced *ath-a-may*). An athame is a ritual knife. It is a short, double-sided blade that is kept dull and is used only to cast a circle or to direct personal power. The athame, or ritual knife if you prefer, has caused much misunderstanding and debate among Witches and the general public.

Most people will get a little wound up if you whip out a double-sided blade and then blandly insist that it is for ceremonial purposes only. You can stand there and tell them until you are blue in the face that the athame is never used to physically cut anything. They will often refuse to believe you. Even the most laid-back and open-minded parent is going to have a hard time with you wielding a double-sided

blade or keeping it in your room. To most nonmagickal people, a double-sided knife is a weapon, plain and simple.

Also from a practical side, many states here in the United States have
strict laws about what is regarded as a legal and an illegal length for a
double- sided blade. If you carry an athame on your person, it may be
considered a concealed weapon. That would not be good. So, after
much internal debate, I decided to be both practical and realistic and
talk about a little known, but much safer, alternative magickal tool that
is also associated with the element of fire: the staff.

How on earth did I ever come up with such an idea? I'll take the
mystery out of this for you right now. As I was planning this chapter, I
decided to do a quick tarot spread and check to see if I was headed in
the right direction. I was particularly concerned with talking about the
traditional magickal tool for the element of fire, for the very reasons
that I listed above.

As I shuffled the cards, a single card fell out and landed faceup on the
floor. I bent over to pick it up and found the Queen of Rods smiling
back at me. In the tarot deck, the suit of Rods is often depicted as a staff
or a large blooming tree branch, and is linked to the element of fire.
The Queen of Rods can represent an enchanting, passionate woman
who is equally at home being both a mother and a career woman. In
my particular deck, the card is illustrated as a red-haired woman holding a blooming staff, surrounded by warm, fiery colors.

"Well, hello," I laughed at the card. The staff it was, then.

The staff is a symbol of strength and leadership. It is traditionally
shoulder height and may be topped with a large crystal point or even a
crystal sphere. Think "walking stick" height. Take a walk and see what
you find. Look for fallen wood—I do not recommend yanking a branch
from a living tree (remember, *harm none*). Make sure that you can identify poison ivy, oak, and sumac, as those vines are usually to be found
growing along the trunks of trees. We don't want you to come home
with a rash.

Refer to the magickal correspondences listed below and look for a
staff—or a wand, for that matter—with some personality. The wood

does not have to be perfectly straight. Some bends and twists in the wood make for an interesting wand or magickal staff. My oldest son turned a favorite walking stick into a magickal staff. He used a twisted, fallen tree branch that he had found out in the woods. He and his father peeled the flaking, dried bark off of the branch and then sealed the wood with a natural wood stain. Refer to the directions on wand construction for directions on how to finish your staff.

THIRTEEN TREES AND THEIR MAGICKAL PROPERTIES

The best place to find the wood for your wand or staff is in nature, somewhere close to home. It is thought that in working with the local natural resources you are strengthening your magickal powers by acknowledging the native energies of the area in which you live. Magickal tools constructed out of these particular woods will carry the associations of the tree it originally came from.

Apple: Love, healing, and garden magick.

Ash: Faerie magick, protection, and healing.

Birch: Goddess magick, women's mysteries.

Cypress: Mystery, protection, recovery, and strength.

Dogwood: Love, safe homes, and family.

Elm: Protection from violent storms, faerie magick.

Hawthorn: Happiness, faerie magick.

Holly: Protection, dream work.

Maple: Love and abundance.

Oak: The God, all-purpose.

Pine: Prosperity and protection.

Rowan (Mountain Ash): All-purpose, a classic Witch's wand.

Witch Hazel: Elemental magick, poetry, fire, and beauty.

The Cup or Cauldron: Water

The cup or cauldron is a Goddess symbol, and a metaphor for emotions and fertility. Another of the customary magickal tools, the cup is actually a cauldron with a stem on it. This traditional tool of Witchcraft and magick has much lore and legend surrounding it. We have the grail that was sought after by the Knights of the Round Table, the Celtic goddess Cerridwen's cauldron of transformation, and the Celtic god Dagda's cauldron of bounty.

Where can you find an inexpensive cauldron? Ignore the occult catalogs and try a camping/fishing type of store instead. A young Witch friend of mine was complaining to me about the price and shipping cost of a small cast-iron cauldron that she had been admiring in an occult catalog. I gladly told her about an identical little iron cauldron for under eight dollars that was for sale in the camping cookware section at a local hunting and outdoor superstore.

Watch arts and crafts festivals or pottery places and see if you can pick up a ceramic goblet. I found an inexpensive blue pottery goblet at a potter's shop a few years ago. There is at least one hand-thrown pottery booth at most festivals or large arts and crafts shows. Check them out. As for making an everyday ceramic or glass cup a little more "magickal," here are some more ideas. Try glass pens and paints and paint the symbol for water onto a clear, large wineglass or mug. Follow the glass paint's manufacturer's directions for baking times to help the paint become permanent on your glass cup. You could glue smooth glass nuggets and "jewels" onto your magickal cup, or decorate the base and stem with small seashells. You will need to use an epoxy-type of glue for these suggestions. Perhaps you could simply keep your eyes open for a large blue "wineglass"-looking type of cup at the store and tie on a few blue ribbons around the stem. Hang a tiny seashell from the ribbons and you're all set.

The Pentacle: Earth

The pentacle represents the earth element. It can be made out of clay, metal, or wood. Its shape is a circle: a flat wooden disc or even a ceramic plate. In the center of the disc is an interwoven, upright, five-pointed star known as the pentagram. The pentagram is an ancient symbol of positive magick. The Witch's pentagram is always point up. Four out of the five points of the pentagram symbolize each of the four elements. The fifth and topmost point of the star stands for the human spirit. The circle that surrounds it binds all of those magickal elements together in harmony.

The old magician Pythagoras called the pentagram the "pentalpha." In medieval Europe, this five-pointed star was sometimes named the "wizard's foot" or the "druid's foot." The ancient Egyptians, Greeks, and Babylonians were all fond of the star symbol, and it was inscribed on doors and windows for protective purposes. The pentagram is actually an endless knot, as it can be drawn without picking the pen up from the paper.

The pentacle is a tool that may be used as a power spot or base from which to charge or bless an object. You could bless or charge crystals or jewelry on your pentacle, or set it up as the central point of your work space as a symbol of positive magick and protection.

Now, for some suggestions on how to make your own pentacle. Check out the local arts and crafts store. See if you can find a ceramic plate and glass paint pens or paint to decorate it with. Make sure that you follow the directions on the paint so your design becomes permanent. Ask someone who works at the arts and crafts store for their advice. (You don't have to tell them that you're making a magickal tool.) Just say you're decorating a ceramic or glass plate as a gift, and ask them what sort of paint they would recommend.

If you are worried about breaking a ceramic pentacle, then consider a wooden one. Usually in the wood shelf and wooden cutout section of the hardware or craft store, you will find small, unfinished wooden plaques. Look for a round one. These are typically made of unfinished pine. Pine is a great wood to use for a pentacle, as it stands for protection and prosperity. If you remember from your correspondence chart in chapter 3, both of those things are associated with the element of earth, as is your pentacle.

Give your future wooden pentacle a light sanding with fine sandpaper to smooth it out, and then transfer your design onto the disc with transfer paper (also found in the arts and crafts store). Either burn the design into the wood with a wood-burning tool, or paint a design onto your pentacle. If you are nervous about painting, consider stenciling a design onto the wood instead. Check the store for celestial stencil patterns. Stencil a large star in the center and decorate around it with moons and suns. How should you design your pentacle? Traditionally, the pentacle has a large pentagram surrounded by a circle in the center of the disc. This pentagram may be surrounded by elemental symbols or personal magickal symbols chosen by the Witch.

I recommend sealing a wooden pentacle with a waterproof finish of some kind. To seal your wooden pentacle after you have decorated it, either stain it with a wood stain or, if you have painted it, then spray the surface with a polyurethane spray. Spray the polyurethane outdoors only, as it has some nasty fumes! If you make your new wooden pentacle waterproof, you can easily clean any spills right up, with no fears of staining or ruining it.

Blessing and Consecrating Your Tools

A Tool Consecration Ritual

Now that you've made your new natural magick accessories, you'll want to bless or consecrate them. When you consecrate an object, you are declaring that this is a special or sacred object. Calling on the God and the Goddess to assist you is a good idea. They'd be happy to help. You may bless the object with each of the four elements, the energies of a full moon, and a bit of your own personal power. By giving a bit of your own personal magick to the tools, you are claiming them. This way, you are making the tools uniquely your own. This gives the tools a sort of magickal brand that will encourage other people to keep their hands off. The tools are for you, and for you alone. Store them in a special place where other people won't be tempted to handle them.

Supplies:

- Your magickal tool(s)

- A half cup of salt or soil

- A small bowl for the soil/salt

- A cup of spring water

- A stick of incense and a holder

- A red votive candle and a votive cup

- Two white candles and the appropriate holder. (The candles represent the God and the Goddess.) Set these up at the back of your work area and use them for illumination. They are also called illuminator candles.

- A lighter or matches

- A safe, flat work space

Perform on the full moon. If possible, perform this consecration outside. If not, find a window that takes in the view of the full moon, and work in front of that. Wherever you are, make sure that the moonbeams shine down on you and your work area.

Arrange the dish of soil/salt, the candle, the cup of water, and the incense and its holder on a flat work surface. Light the red candle and the incense. Light the illuminator candles and ask the God and Goddess to bless you, in your own words. Ground and center. Then begin.

Here is a consecration charm:

On this evening of the full moon glowing so white,

I ask the Lord and Lady to assist me tonight.

(Hold up the tool. Let the moonlight fall across it.)

I bless this tool by the powers of earth

(sprinkle a little soil or salt on the tool)

and water

(sprinkle a bit of the water on the tool)

with fire

(hold the tool above the candle flame and pass it around

in a clockwise motion)

and air.

(pass the tool through the incense smoke)

May I work magick with this tool wisely.

Let my spells be both honorable and fair.

Set the tool aside. If you are consecrating more than one, repeat the procedure with each tool. When you have blessed each tool with the four elements, then continue.

Lift your hands up and imagine that the moon is filling you from head to heels with her light and magick. Now raise your personal power and lay your hands upon your tool(s). Transfer a little bit of personal power to your tools.

Close by saying:

I claim these magick tools as my own,

and I vow to harm none,

I thank the Lord and Lady for their help.

Now my spell is done!

Place your hands on the earth or floor, and ground and center your-self. Draw up stabilizing energy from the earth. Take a few deep breaths and blow them out slowly. Rise to your feet after a moment or two and clean up your work space. If you choose, you may let the illu-minator candles continue to burn for a while. (Remember to keep an eye on them.) Pinch them out when you are finished with the cleanup. You may reuse the illuminator candles whenever you wish. Set them up on your work area to represent the God and the Goddess, and your connection to them both.

Magickal Work Spaces and Altars

Here is something for you to consider: how about setting up a perma-nent work area in which to perform your magick? The altar can be con-sidered another kind of a tool, as it is a place to work your spells and to display a natural symbol of each of the four elements. In this personal, special place, you could celebrate your connection to the elements and to the God and the Goddess. The altar, or a magickal work space, is a spot that is reserved for you to perform your indoor charms and spells. A Witch's altar does not have to be gothic and grim. If you are clever, you could probably leave your altar set up most of the time and no one will even notice it.

Where should you set it up? Try using your nightstand or a corner of your dresser. What should you place on your magickal work area? An altar usually has a representation of each of the four elements. A God and Goddess symbol of some kind is featured, and the work space has a source of illumination, so that you can see what you're doing.

For your natural magick altar, try using a crystal cluster to represent the element of earth, or even a houseplant. A fallen feather that you found could signify the element of air. You could set out a red candle for fire, or, if you're not allowed to burn candles in your room, then try adding a lava rock or a small dragon figurine. For the element of water, a seashell or two will fit the bill nicely.

As to your representation of the God and Goddess, try looking for magickally themed greeting cards with attractive artwork of the Goddess and God on them. Pick up an inexpensive frame to display it in, and set that up there. Or you could set out some oak leaves and a few acorns to represent the God, and a white flower in a vase for the Goddess.

For your source of illumination, you can go with candles, if you have a safe place to burn them, or a small accessory lamp with a low wattage lightbulb. You could always decorate the little lamp with a star-painted shade, or use some celestial design. Try using attractive stickers to decorate a plain lamp base. You could find a lamp with a nature theme on it, like leaves and ferns. Come on, use your imagination. What kind of nifty natural things are you imagining for your magickal work space?

A friend of mine has her altar displayed on her dresser in her bedroom. Her dresser is an antique that has small shelves built into the mirror that attaches to the dresser. On her little shelves she has a gold candle for the God and a silver candle to represent the Goddess. Sitting on a separate shelf is an incense holder and her perfume bottles for the element of air. A blue ceramic celestial-theme coffee mug is displayed on another, to signify the element of water. There are a few candles in pretty glass holders for fire, and some rocks and crystals clustered around the candles to symbolize the element of earth. These candles and stones are snuggled together on the last shelf and it completes her altar setup. This altar display has remained pretty much the same since she was a teen and living at home. Now that she has her own place, she still enjoys setting her work space up the same way. This is her personal magickal tradition.

I bet that you're trying to figure out what my altar looks like, aren't you? Okay, I'll give. The one in my room is on top of a five-foot-tall magickal cabinet. The display itself looks like a nice arrangement of fun and funky things—and no, it does not scream out *Witch!* when you walk in the room. It is much more subtle. Arranged on the top of the cabinet are a couple of small framed pictures of different aspects of the Goddess. One is a small three-by-five-inch print of the moon goddess Selene, and the other is a lovely stylized picture of Isis. In the center of the cabinet's surface is a small stained-glass fan lamp that I made years ago. The glass in the lamp is iridescent blue, white, and yellow. The pattern is a smiling crescent moon against a dark blue sky, with a lone, five-pointed yellow star. It uses a nightlight bulb to light up and I click that on when I am working. It gives me plenty of light, and the glass illuminates beautifully.

I have a small piece of deer antler that represents the God. I have a tiny cauldron just big enough to hold a tealight, and another tealight candleholder that has the word "magick" etched all over it. Let's see, what else is up there . . . an incense holder, a dish of salt, a seashell, and a few clusters of quartz crystals are also arranged on my cabinet. Does the setup stay the same? Nope. I move things around and rearrange them from time to time.

Usually around Beltane I set out a faerie statue that my husband gave me for my birthday. The faerie is sleeping and a little accompanying life-sized frog figurine guards her. Next to that sits a framed card featuring a faerie dancing with butterflies. Both the faerie and the framed card are all in shades of yellow, so it is attractive and springlike when it is all displayed together.

Now, before someone gets all in a snit about me having an indoor work space, let me point out that sometimes even I can't work outside. During the winter months it's just too cold. Or if we are having nasty weather and thunderstorms, then I'm pretty much stuck inside. We get a lot of those spring and summer weather tantrums here in the Midwest, you know. It's not exactly smart to be outside during inclement weather. I try to work outside in the garden or yard whenever I can for the most part—weather permitting—and so should you.

Having a little magickal work space in your room is a constant way to keep you connected to the elements and to the Lord and Lady, no matter what is happening outside. By setting up a little altar full of accessories and images of the natural energies of magick, you are bringing those spiritual energies of nature inside and keeping them close to you.

As we close up this chapter, I want you to remember that fancy tools and elaborate altars do not the better Witch make. Keep things simple and natural. These tools and accessories are only meant to help you focus your energies and to strengthen your work with the elements and the powers of nature. The magickal energy that they amplify or help you to direct has only one source. Don't let yourself get so wrapped up in all of the paraphernalia that you forget the important stuff. After all, the true magickal tools are your mind and your heart.

Remember . . . the magick is inside of you.

IV
Walking the Path
of Natural Magick

Go confidently in the direction
of your **DREAMS**
LIVE the life you've imagined.
—HENRY DAVID THOREAU

TEN

Properly Prepared

Well, we are just bouncing right along, aren't we? You are learning the basics of natural magick and are beginning to understand the elemental energies and the mechanics of spellcasting with some earthy and simple supplies. So what's with this "properly prepared" chapter? I bet you're thinking that if you weren't prepared to learn about the Craft, you wouldn't have gotten this far. And, in a way, that is true. However, I want to talk to you about the reality of Witchcraft and the inevitable changes that come into your life when you practice magick. A favorite Craft chant of mine goes like this: "She changes everything she touches, and everything she touches changes."

Recently I was reminded of this situation when a young college-aged friend of mine, Noire, became spooked after a sabbat celebration that had been held at my house. Noire had been investigating magick for some time before she began to work with my group. She had studied on her own and was fascinated by the prospect of working with the Goddess. For Noire, coming to the sabbat celebrations was about learning more about the religious aspect of Wicca. She also enjoyed learning how to cast a circle and how to work magick with a group of people.

My circle of ladies was celebrating the sabbat of Ostara, the spring equinox. We had dyed eggs with each other and held a quiet and informal ritual to celebrate. It was a small group that night, as one circlemate was out of town on a business trip and another was home with a couple of sick children. One of the ladies had taken us through a relaxing guided meditation during our ritual celebration and now that the ritual was finished for the evening, we were all hanging out in the living room, kicking back, laughing, snacking, and talking.

One of the visitors to our circle, named Raven, was sitting on the floor and complaining of a nasty headache. As Witches tend to do, my friend Nicole offered to help her out. Nicole wanted to see if she could remove the headache by using Reiki. This is a healing technique that works primarily with moving universal energy through the body. Nicole was beginning her Reiki classes and was eager to try out her new skills on a volunteer.

Nicole stood behind Raven and began to silently work on ridding her of the headache. Noire had been sitting a few feet behind and off to the side of Raven. She was slouching in a rocking chair and watching the goings-on with some interest. Suddenly, I watched Noire's eyes pop wide in her face, and she scrambled out of the chair and over to the other side of the room next to me.

"Felt that energy, did you?" I asked.

"Holy cow," was Noire's shaken reply.

Raven and Nicole smiled over at her, and Raven announced that her headache had considerably lessened. Nicole quietly finished up her healing, patted Raven on the shoulder, and then strolled over to the couch. Noire looked at Nicole like she had never seen her before.

"Are you having an Oh-my-god, this-stuff-is-real moment?" I teased her.

"I felt that," Noire had yet to calm down. "I mean, I *really* felt that."

"Well, I imagine so, as she was moving energy around," I pointed out.

"Yeah, but this was incredibly strong," Noire said, with very big eyes.

Nicole spoke up. "You said that you could feel the energy in the circle during the ritual on Samhain. Was this so different?" She looked at Noire and smiled gently.

Noire didn't answer, but she was unusually quiet for the remainder of the evening.

Much to my surprise, this really shook Noire, to the point that she dropped out of the group for a little while. There were no hard feelings. Unfortunately, I have seen this kind of thing happen before. As is often the case, it is one thing to read books on the subject and quite another to actually practice Witchcraft. For some people, the discovery that they can actually feel the manipulation of energy in a healing or during a circlecasting, or that their cast spells really work, is quite a shocker. That forces them to look both at themselves and the world around them differently. It forces them to deal with change—and change is terrifying for some people.

Recently engaged, and trying to decide whether or not to move out on her own, Noire was in the middle of a tumultuous time. When the spellwork that she had done, asking for the courage to be strong and to deal with the new facets of her life, actually began to manifest change . . . well, she got a little nervous.

Sadly, for some folks, both young and old alike, staying in an unhappy job, emotionally abusive home environment, or in a—Goddess forbid—physically abusive relationship is less frightening than having to actually accept and live with the transformation of their life, even if the change is for the better. Their magick has suddenly forced them to deal with the situation and the inevitable transformation that their spell has wrought.

Noire took some time off from magick and reevaluated why she was interested in the Craft in the first place. She talked to her fiancé and then thought long and hard about where she wanted to go from here. And she asked herself some pretty tough questions.

Did she start to study magick so she could feel special? No. Was it so she could wear all the pretty silver magickal jewelry? Nope. Did she get involved in the group so she could hang out on the full moon and boast to her nonmagickal friends that she knew some "real Witches"? Of course not.

Noire became interested in the Craft because she wanted to learn more about the Goddess and because she needed to gain a sense of self-empowerment. When Noire began to realize how real and true magick could be, she wisely took a good, hard look at herself and what she hoped to accomplish. Noire's perception of herself and the world had changed. No matter where she goes from here, she will be a very different young woman. Noire sat down and decided that she was prepared to learn more. Now that she recognized the energies of nature, she decided to challenge herself by studying and discovering more about the elements and natural magick.

About a month later, she contacted me and asked if she could join the group the next time that we got together to celebrate the sabbat of Beltane. We talked for a bit about her soul searching, and I asked her if she was sure that she would be comfortable. She assured me that she was.

As the group gathered together in my garden and began to set up our circle, everyone sort of drifted toward the quarter or direction that they normally call. I usually call in the element of earth, so I moved to the northern quarter. Amy strolled over to the east, for air, and Nicole headed to the south to call in the element of fire.

There were four other members present, and any of them were welcome to stand in the western quarter to call in the element of water. Actually, the two younger teen members, my daughter and Amy's, were playfully debating between themselves who would get to have the honors.

Then Noire spoke up, firmly and with confidence. "I'll just take my usual spot in the west. I'd like to call in water." Noire strode over to the western direction of the circle and planted her feet with a serious expression on her face. She tossed her dark red hair behind her and turned to face that direction, silently preparing herself.

The group fell silent and we all began to grin with pride at one another. This was quite a change from the Noire of the last get-together. I heard someone whisper, "You go, girl!"

Noire turned back around and faced the group. "Are we ready?"

"Yes," I answered her. "I think you really are."

Witchcraft is real. The elemental energies that you call on are real. Working magick will bring true change into your life. Remember what we discussed way back in chapter 1? "Magick is the art and science of affecting positive change in your life." If you are going to work magick and cast spells to bring about an improvement, then be prepared to deal with that change when it arrives. This is part of being properly prepared.

Circle Casting 101

Now, if you are thinking to yourself, *Gee, she's been talking about casting circles but she hasn't giving me any information on this topic yet* . . . Just hang on, because I'm about to. I want to make sure that you are at least familiar with some terms and ideas before I launch into this topic.

This circlecasting business can be confusing for newer Witches. What am I saying—it can be confusing for *all* Witches! Half of the time, when a spell or charm is listed in a book, there is no mention of circlecasting in the directions (I didn't give you any in this book, either). Do you know what this means? It means that you are going to have to decide for yourself when and if it is appropriate to cast a circle during your magick. Got you again, didn't I?

To cast a circle or not to cast, that is the question. Here is a subject that is hotly debated among Witches and other magick users. "When is it appropriate to cast a magick circle?" There are some texts that insist that absolutely no magick, of any kind, should ever be performed without being properly prepared with the protection of a magick circle. Some magickal people insist that a circle should only be cast when there is a serious ritual or important "big guns" type of magick being performed. Others rarely cast a magick circle at all, unless they are celebrating a sabbat or working with a large group of people. Well, if that isn't enough to boggle your mind, then I don't know what is.

Magick is a very personal and individual thing. You get to decide for yourself how you want to work it. My friend Amy, for example, casts a circle only rarely. Her exceptions are when she is working with a large group or if she is performing a banishing (the removal of a very negative situation). When and if she does formally cast a circle, then she silently casts one by using the force and power of visualization and her imagination. Amy just steps up, centers herself, calls on the elements, and gets to work. No nonsense, no props . . . just *boom!* And there it is. So, you may be wondering, if it is "just that easy," then why do Witches mess with casting a circle at all? And here would be the answer.

When a Witch casts a circle, they are creating a temporary and formal sacred space in which to communicate with deity and work their magick. Just as some religious groups go to a church, mosque, or synagogue to worship and pray, Witches erect a circle to make a temporary sacred place in which to pray and perform their magick. Their circles are built by using the powers of nature, in harmony with the four elements.

Working Within a Circle: Why, How, and When?

Witches use the shape of a circle for many reasons; here are just a few. The circle is a sacred shape. It may represent the cycle of the seasons, the sun, and the moon. It can symbolize a sacred hoop or a medicine wheel. A circle can also be used to describe the wheel of the year. Also, the circle is historically associated with the idea of a magickally protected or consecrated space—a sort of holy ground for ritual, where magick and worship takes place. Take, for example, stone circles in England, like Stonehenge and Avebury. Even though no one knows for sure what took place at Stonehenge, or why exactly it was built, it is widely believed and accepted that worship of some kind took place there.

So, how *exactly* do you cast a circle? There are about as many different ways to cast as there are Witches. But, before you roll your eyes in frustration, let me give you a few examples of simple circlecastings. We have actually touched on this topic a few times already, in chapter 2 with the Blue Shield of Fire Visualization, and in the fire element chapter. Remember the meditation and the teen who cast the circle with their staff for protection?

A circle may be cast physically by the act of introducing a natural representation of each of the four elements to the designated area. It is widely agreed upon that a circle should be cast with the natural energies of earth, air, fire, and water. You are already familiar with these natural energies. Why not work with them?

Unless you are in serious trouble, try not to use your own personal energy to create a barrier. If you feel compelled to, then go ahead and carefully reinforce the circle with your own personal power, just like in the fire element meditation. But don't be surprised if you are really tired after you are finished with your magickal work. Tossing down personal power zaps your strength for a short while. You may need to have a snack and take a quick nap afterwards. It will be easier and less taxing for you if you create the circle using the elemental energies of nature instead.

How big should the circle be? Well, again, that is up to you. Some folks say nine feet across, others say six. A good rule of thumb is to give yourself plenty of room to move around in. My personal circles usually are four to five feet in diameter. If I am working with my group, we usually cast a circle big enough to take up the entire living room. If we are outside in the garden, then we cast the circle about nine to ten feet in diameter, as this leaves everyone with room to comfortably move around.

A Teen Witch's Elemental Circle Casting

Let's give you a visual here. We will say that Brittany, a Teen Witch friend of mine, is casting a circle. The first thing that she will do is to prepare her work area. If she is inside, working in her room, then it is a neat and clean environment. That way, she remains more focused. Less clutter equals less distraction. (She's a smart Witch, that Brittany.) If she is working outside on the back patio or in the yard, then she makes sure that things are tidy out there as well. Since the weather is nice this evening, let's put Brittany in her backyard for this demonstration.

Brittany takes a moment and aligns herself with the four directions, or quarters. Each of the four quarters represents a natural element. As you recall from the elemental correspondence charts in Part II of this book, the direction north is aligned with the element of earth. The east corresponds with the element of air. The south represents the element of fire and, lastly, the west symbolizes the element of water.

Brittany decides to make this circle about six feet in diameter. So, in the center of her future circle, she has set up a small table with all of her supplies on it. For her circlecasting she has gathered a small bowl full of rich topsoil, a red candle, a lighter, an incense stick, and a ceramic goblet full of spring water. First, she lights the incense and the candle. Once the joss stick is burning nicely, she blows out the flame and then fans a bit of the scented smoke over her body to cleanse herself of all negativity. This procedure is called smudging (see chapter 4). Now Brittany takes a moment and gathers her thoughts and centers herself. She breathes out and in, slowly. She takes nice, even breaths and imagines that all around her is calm and peaceful. When Brittany feels that she is ready, she begins.

Facing the direction north, she holds up her dish of soil and says, "By the powers of earth, strength, and stability, I cast this circle." She turns to the right and walks around her circle in a clockwise direction (Witches call this direction *deosil*). As she goes, Brittany sprinkles a tiny bit of soil around the imagined perimeter of her circle. The soil that she is lightly sprinkling on the ground physically represents the element of earth.

Witch Tip: You may notice in various magickal books that it recommends using salt for the element of earth. If you are working inside, a small amount of salt is less noticeable and much easier to clean up. However, if you are casting this circle out-of-doors and you use salt, it may kill the grass. So, be a thoughtful Witch and use a small amount of soil outdoors instead of salt. A good rule of thumb to follow is soil = outside, salt = inside.

After setting the dish down on her table, Brittany turns to face the east. She picks up a fragrant, smoldering incense stick. She holds it up and announces, "By the powers of air, knowledge, and inspiration, I cast this circle," and, turning to the right, she carries the smoking incense around the edge of her circle to represent the presence of the element of air. She stops by her table, sets the stick back into its holder, and exchanges the incense for the lit candle.

To call in the element of fire, she starts in the south. Brittany holds up the lit, red candle and calls out, "By the powers of fire, protection, and passion, I cast this circle." Then, turning to the right again, the candle is carried around the boundary, also in a clockwise direction. Brittany cruises by the table and switches the candle for the goblet of water.

Finally, Brittany faces the west. She holds up the goblet of water and speaks, "By the powers of water, love, and emotion, I cast this circle." Always moving clockwise (deosil), she turns to the right and sprinkles drops of liquid on the ground as she walks the edge of the circle.

Brittany now moves to the center of her circle and sets down the goblet. She takes a moment to visualize all of the four elements humming around her in a beautiful, multicolored ring. She holds her hands out to her sides, palms up, and declares, "By the powers of earth, air, fire, and water, this circle is sealed."

That was simple enough. When Brittany is finished with her magickal work, she will take down the circle by walking around the boundaries in a counterclockwise direction (Witches call this direction *widdershins*). Starting in the west, she will turn and walk to the left, going to the south, next to the east, and finally to the north. As she walks the circle, she will quietly but firmly say, "The circle is open but unbroken. Merry meet, merry part, and merry meet again." Moving back to the center where her table is, Brittany will ground and center, then snuff out the candle and the incense. Then she will clean up and put away her supplies. That is one example of a circlecasting that uses the natural powers of the four elements.

A Teen Witch's Elemental Magick

How about a guy's opinion? Let's talk to Jake for a while. Jake and his mother both practice Wicca. Jake is eighteen and a very elemental and down-to-earth type of guy. Jake really doesn't care for formal Witchcraft; instead, he prefers to work primarily with the elements and with natural magick. For Jake, the God and Goddess are represented all around him, within the natural world. He follows his heart and his instincts with quiet confidence and belief. He informs me that, unless he is working with a group, he does not cast a circle at all. Jake does, however, get a kick out of working weather magick and calling for a freshening breeze or a gentle rain shower during the long, hot, summer months. This is his specialty.

When the mood is upon him, Jake quietly stands outside and connects his spirit with nature. He closes his eyes and imagines that a cool breeze and life-giving rain will come. He links with the elements of the earth by feeling the ground beneath his bare feet and the strength of the sun beating down on his head. He intensely visualizes the soft change in the weather that he is working for, and raises up and then releases his personal power. Usually, within a day, the soothing weather changes that he has been working for arrive. For this young man, all of nature is a sacred space, so casting a circle is redundant, in his opinion. On a funny personal note, as I wrote this section, it began to thunder and an unexpected, gentle spring rain moved in. Wow . . . he is good.

So, you see, it is truly up to you. Go with what you like and research this topic for yourself. Being a properly prepared Witch is studying, learning, and then deciding for yourself how you wish to perform natural magick. Try a spell within a cast circle, and then do a spell without a circle. Try the directions for a natural magick circle or use one of the circle chants that is listed in italics below. Keep notes and see how things develop.

Magick is so much more than just collecting books. Take what you learn from them and then put those positive lessons into practice. Make your magick personal, individual, and have fun! Remember to harm none, and to follow your own instincts. Use your brains and always, always, listen to your heart.

CIRCLE CHANTS

(Repeat these three times.)

I am a circle

within a circle

With no beginning

and without ending.

Air I am, fire I am,

water, earth and spirit I am.

Coming Full Circle

As for myself, the basic guidelines that I follow for a circlecasting are these:

- If I am not at my home and I perform magick, I always cast a circle. (This makes the new space that I am working in sacred and protected.)

- Should I be performing a rather serious spell, such as a healing, a banishing, or the return of a stolen item and a call for justice, then I will be more formal and cast a circle. (The keywords here are *serious* and *formal*.)

- If I am working with a group or my circle mates, we cast a circle together without exception, as a symbol of unity and friendship.

I do *not* cast a circle under these circumstances:

- If I am in a wild place in nature, like walking through the woods or kneeling next to a spring. This is already a sacred place.

- If I am performing a simple charm or spell at home or in the garden. Then I do not require the use of a formal circle to create a sacred space, because I consider my entire house and yard already to be both a hallowed and protected area.

How can I possibly do that, you may ask? I consider it to be a sacred space because I made it that way myself by blessing, cleansing, and consecrating the entire house and yard.

Outdoor Sacred Spaces

To create a sacred space is to make an area of your home or yard into a permanently prepared spot in which to perform your magick. Usually this is accomplished by bringing in something from each of the four elements and by blessing and consecrating the area. This would be a process similar to blessing your tools, such as we discussed back in chapter 9. After the area has been blessed, then you create a marker for the area. It can be anything from an inexpensive garden figurine of a faerie or even a statue of a goddess. A small garden sign that reads "Enchanted Garden" would be fun. How about a Green Man mask? Or you could set up a discreet little display of magickal objects.

For example, you could keep your sacred space marker really small. Pile up some smooth decorative stones into a pyramid for the element of earth. Stick a feather in the center of the pile for the element of air. Set off to the side of this little stack of stones a lava rock to represent fire. Then set a seashell on the opposite side of the arrangement to represent the element of water.

Use your imagination. Perhaps you will want to plant a tree or some perennial flowers that will come back and bloom for you every year. Maybe you'll want to set a stepping-stone into the yard or garden as your marker. They have neat kits at most arts and crafts stores to make your own decorated stepping-stones. (Just imagine what you could do with those!) You could even make four different stepping-stones, one for each element. You could decorate them with different colored mosaic glass or draw magickal symbols on them. *Ooh, the possibilities . . .*

Now that we've gotten you to think about it for a moment, let's give you some brief but bewitching charms and blessings to use to consecrate your new outdoor sacred magickal space. Immediately following these is an outline for your ritual. I am giving you an outline only because you should have enough magickal knowledge by now to set this up and perform it without being led by the hand.

Elemental Blessing

Gnomes and faeries, dragons and undines too.

Hear my magickal call from me to you.

Lend your powers to mine, guard well this space.

As together we bless this magick place.

Lord and Lady Blessing

The Lady of the Moon and the Lord of the Sun,

help me to work magick wisely, and to harm none.

Assist me now, smile down on this sacred space,

as with your guidance I bless this magick place.

Consecrating Your Outdoor Space:
A Ritual Outline

Choose your sacred space marker or markers, and gather your supplies and get them ready to go. If you should choose to take candles outside, than I urge you to be especially careful with them. Keep them inside of a holder or a large bowl while working outdoors. Never leave any burning candles unattended.

- Set up the area. If you have to pull a few weeds or pick up any stuff left lying around, this should be done ahead of time. Make sure that it is neat and clean. Less distractions means more focused ability.

- Choose your time, either on the evening of a full moon or in the daytime when the sun is directly overhead. You could also try working at sunset or at sunrise. These in-between times are thought to be very magickal, as dawn and dusk are neither night nor day.

- Cast a circle. Either use the directions listed above or use your imagination and be spontaneous.

- Recite one of the blessings listed above or make up your own.

- Set up your marker.

- Raise up your personal power and then lay your hands onto the soil and exchange some energy with the area.

- Ground and center. Thank the elementals and tell them to return safely to their homes. Thank the Lord and Lady for their help.

- Open the circle by saying,

The circle is open but unbroken.

Merry meet, merry part, and merry meet again.

Lastly, remember this. The single most important and powerful aspect of turning an area into a sacred space would be you—you and your magickal will and positive intentions. A Witch that is properly prepared, thoughtful, and creative is a tough combination to beat. Go ahead and figure out what you would like to do with your own personal outdoor sacred space. Have fun and be artistic. Draw your inspiration for the sacred space from the beauty of nature. I'll bet that you can come up with some wonderful ideas on your own.

ELEVEN

Lessons Learned on Living a Magickal Life

Life has its ups and downs; how you handle yourself as you travel through the bumps and dips in the road is what develops character. In reality, living a magickal life is nothing like the movies. Take, for instance, the 1996 movie *The Craft*—that film opened quite the can of worms in the magickal community.

Some folks thought it was campy and fun and a great example of the magickal rule of three. Other folks booed and hissed rather loudly over the film, claiming that it was too sensational and too "Hollywood." They also felt that it was a negative stereotype of Witches and magick.

In my opinion, movies like *The Craft* are meant to be taken as fun and entertaining. They are not training films. They were not meant to be used as a primer into magick. In its own way, though, the movie had a good, solid lesson. The overall message of the film was to abide by the rule of three. My favorite line from the film is when the shopkeeper tells the girls, "True magick is neither black nor white. It is both because nature is both. . . . The only good or bad is in the heart of the Witch. Life keeps a balance on its own."

Well, *there* is a familiar theme that I've been harping on for a while. And you should have this down cold. Don't play around with or dabble in magick. It is not meant to be used as a joke or as something to do because you feel lonely, bored, or want to get even with someone. If you purposely harm or manipulate another with magick, you will be paid back in turn. The characters in the film paid the price for their manipulations and, when all was said and done, only the girl who was the most honorable was left standing with her gifts intact.

So what does that have to do with you? We've spent the last ten chapters exploring natural magick, the God and Goddess, and how to work with the energies of nature. You should have many new ideas, gained some experience, and have a better understanding about what natural magick truly is. Recently, a young Witch named Willow and I had a talk about what living a magickal life is really all about. Willow's mom and I are circle mates. Over the last year I have watched this young lady grow and mature. Both Willow and Kat take turns assisting during circle meetings. Occasionally one may call a quarter, or they help out by riding herd on the various younger siblings or babies that come to our circle with their mothers from time to time.

"It's not all black candles and weird clothes, you know," Willow states firmly. "Magick and Witchcraft are used only for positive actions and intentions." She continues, saying, "Witchcraft isn't what I thought it would be. It's better and more realistic."

"You mean natural?" I asked her.

"Yes," she nods to me, and then collars her younger brother as he zooms past her. "That's it exactly. "

Now that you are beginning to live the life of a Witch, let's take a realistic look at everyday life and problems that you may encounter. More importantly, let's discuss how to handle these potential problems ethically, by using a sense of humor and, most importantly, a sense of honor. Let's talk about personal integrity and magickal responsibility.

In my kitchen hangs a little wooden Halloween plaque. The scene painted on the plaque shows a full moon rising behind a black cat. The cat has huge yellow eyes and all around the sides of the plaque, over and over, it asks, "Are you a good Witch or a bad Witch?"

Ah . . . the eternal debate. When someone asks me that question, I usually look them straight in the eye and reply in my best imitation of Glinda, from *The Wizard of Oz*, "Only bad Witches are ugly." Fairy tales aside, the way you look has nothing to do with it. *Of course* I believe myself to be a good Witch. Let's see . . . I haven't run amok throwing out black magick curses and hexes for days now. I mean, honestly, who has the time? A favorite, traditional Craft saying goes like this:

"Eight words the Wiccan Rede fulfill, an' it harm none, do as you will."

The Rede is both simple and complex. As Witches and natural magicians, we understand that what we send out will return to us three times over, be it bad or good. This is the law of three. Both the Rede and the law of three are among the first lessons Witches should learn and always hold close to their hearts.

Shades of Gray

Well, then, where did all the hoopla about white and black magick begin? *White magick*, as it is sometimes referred to, is utilized to bring about positive change for ourselves and our loved ones. Black magick, on the other hand, is a touchy subject. Most Witches will agree that black magick falls under the category of performing malignant spells on purpose—using magick for intended harm and for destructive reasons. Interfering with another's free will and magickal manipulation are off-limits and may also be considered black magick. A Witch should never use their powers to harm or deliberately frighten anyone.

Sometimes you will hear people talk about gray magick. Gray magick is, naturally, somewhere in between black and white. Bindings, banishings, and extreme protective magicks are all examples of gray magick. Accepting payment for spellcasting would fall under gray magick as well (a definite no-no). Another school of thought believes that gray magicks occur under the circumstances of glamouries as well.

A glamoury is a deliberate magickal transformation of your personality or appearance for the purpose of manipulating another's perception of you. Remember chapter 4 and the air meditation? Glamouries are usually a positive thing. However, it doesn't take much to nudge a glamoury into something less than beneficial and more like a tricky advantage for the spellcaster. It depends on how far you take it. You may have to adjust the volume, so to speak, unless you are looking for trouble.

What I mean by that is to keep the glamoury to a minimum, or you might accidentally catch the attention of people that you were not interested in, or ever would be. Like your best friend's boyfriend. Yikes! That would be bad.

But what *really* happens to you if you mess up and make a bad judgment call? Many people over the years, both adults and teens, have asked me about this topic. They also want to know why no one talks about this. The reason you do not see a lot of information about this in various Craft books is because it is a sticky and controversial subject. Every magick user has their own opinion on magickal mistakes and negative magick. As do I.

So what if you do lose your temper and have a magickal misfire— what happens then? Do you fall into those thousand shades of gray somewhere in between white and black magick? Can you ever get back out of the dark side and back into the light? The answer is, "Yes, young Skywalker, you can." Sometimes the God and Goddess, in all their infinite wisdom, are merely waiting to teach us a lesson. You just may not enjoy these lessons very much.

There are two sides to magick, and to our own personalities: a light side and a shadow side. Learning to accept and work in balance with our shadow side is important. By curbing your temper and other, more unattractive qualities, you gain power and wisdom. This is what we should aspire to. The shadow side is a very real part of us. Respect your shadow side; know its strengths and its weaknesses. Don't ignore or deny its existence, otherwise it might come back and bite you in the you-know-what.

A Lesson from the Shadow Side

I once learned a hard lesson from my shadow side, by blithely assuming that my temper was always under my control when it came to magick. Many years of magickal experience didn't keep me from making a mistake. It can happen.

I had taken a job working in a garden center. A great job, I thought at first. Nice boss, great pay. There was one problem: the owner's seventy-year-old parents, we'll call them Mom and Pop. They were hateful to all of the employees, shouting and cursing at them in front of the customers—especially the teens who worked there for the summer, they really caught a lot of it.

On a particularly hot and nasty day, with threatening thunderstorms, Mom and Pop had been in all their glory. I had been the sole receiver of all their malignant attention. The teens who worked there were literally hiding, and who could blame them? It had been an awful day and, to cap it off, Mom and Pop informed me, in colorful terms, that if it had been up to them, I never would have been hired. I was hurt and furious, both for myself and the other employees. No one deserves that type of treatment. I could feel myself losing my composure as I fought to stand there and appear professional. I hadn't been that angry in a long time. But even as I maintained my outward composure, I felt my magickal one slipping.

My blood pounded in my ears and my stomach twisted painfully. I remember trying desperately to ground and center, but I was too angry, thinking how much I really hated those two. They were bitter and cruel. As they stood and argued over what errand to go run, I thought to myself, "Just go. Pick on each other for a change and leave us alone. Find something to keep you busy and don't come back." As they left, I felt a tremendous rush of energy leave with them, and it had come from me. I sat down, shaken and spent. "Oh boy," I thought. "What just happened here?"

A half-hour later, the phone rang. Mom and Pop had been in a car accident. The roads were slick from the rain, and when they swerved to avoid hitting a stopped car, they drove off the road and into a steep ditch. They were both uninjured and were calling to ask us to send a tow truck and to let us know that they were okay. By all accounts, they were still arguing as they sat there, waiting to be pulled out. Their car only had to have a few minor repairs.

I often warn my teens about the law of three. What goes around, comes around. Anger and magick is a bad combination. No, it hadn't been deliberate on my part, but I know better than to let my magickal temper slip. Telling myself it was just karma from all the nasty things the older couple did to the employees didn't make me feel any better. It made me feel worse. I sent a prayer to the Goddess in thanks that they hadn't been hurt and then waited to see if there would be any karmic repercussions. I didn't have to wait long. A Druid friend of mine once said to me that karma was mess because karma splashes. How very true.

The next week, both of my family's cars broke down within a thirty-six-hour time period of each other. We were able to repair one car ourselves, but the other car needed a mechanic. Many of the electric systems were shot and the repair bill was very expensive. Basically, it boils down to this: I screwed up, and my family and I paid the price.

Maybe the Goddess was giving me a none-too-gentle smack upside the head, reminding me that with power comes responsibility. This is a lesson that still makes me stop and consider the possible outcome of each and every spell that I cast today. I keep a very tight grip on the reins of my magick when my temper is involved. I won't go near my tools and I give myself at least a twenty-four-hour cooling-off period. No more nasty repercussions thataway.

Acting responsibly is a vital part of wielding power. Being able to protect and defend yourself and your family without causing harm to others is the real trick. If we feel that our personal safety, jobs, or our loved ones are threatened, that's when our strongest emotions are involved. Be wise and think before you throw around magick. You can do it. It takes a measure of calmness and control, not anger or thoughts of revenge. Magickal power without control becomes a stupidly dangerous thing, as my story illustrates.

Yes, I can admit that I have made mistakes. (Pay attention to what I'm saying here and don't make the same one.) Part of growing and living is making mistakes, learning from them, and then moving on. Realizing this is a key element in magick. This is an important part of your magickal training and yet another one of those elements that separates the wide-eyed teenage dabbler from the more experienced Teen Witch.

So, how 'bout it? Are you a good Witch or a bad Witch? As for myself, some days it's hard to tell. When I'm hollering at my teenagers to pick up their rooms or to get the dirty socks off the living room floor, my three teens will swear to you that I'm a bad Witch . . . only an evil woman would make them clean their rooms, after all.

Natural Magick Solutions

The practical and natural magick that deals with the everyday difficulties of life and the not-so-average day-to-day problems should not require you to run to your bookshelf every time for books and spells. Memorize some simple spells and a circle casting.

Come on, no complaining. You can do it. Be bold and daring! True magick is all about desire and will. If you need to tap into magick when you have a specific problem, don't waste time by thumbing through your books. Some magickal knowledge and simple charms you should memorize. Then they are available to you at all times—because you never know when you might have to quickly call on them.

For example, when my daughter's flute was stolen right out from under her as she stood putting away things in her locker, we did all the basic, mundane things. We searched the school. Then we talked to all the custodians and asked them to keep an eye out for her flute case. We notified the principal and asked her band director if anyone had turned in a "lost" flute—all to no avail.

Her principal smugly informed me that they had never had an instrument stolen from a student at the school before. He was sure it was simply . . . misplaced. Now, I know my daughter. She is relentless about her personal belongings. As Kat cried and insisted that she did not leave it laying around anywhere, I believed her.

After a long holiday weekend, come Tuesday morning, the flute was still missing. It was my day off, so I called the school office and spoke to one of the secretaries, and asked her if there had been any news. She told me no, and that everyone was still searching; there wasn't anything else to do but wait and hope. I knew that the longer amount of time that went by, the less chance we had of recovering the flute. I hung up the phone grim, determined, and feeling a sense of urgency. There was no time to waste. I had to do something to help, and I had to do it right now. Well, was I a Witch or not?

I had no fresh herbs on hand, as it was winter, but I wasn't about to let that stop me. I had just purchased a large vanilla-scented pillar candle. There it sat on top of the wood-burning stove in my living room, unlit and unused. As you recall from the section in chapter 5 on candle magick, the scent of vanilla is used in magick for love and desire. It can also be used to focus mental powers.

Well, hello there, I thought as I picked up that candle. *Hmm, let's see. . . I love my daughter and she desires to get her flute back.* I could tap into universal mental powers to get the thief to 'fess up about the location of the flute and, if I was really careful, I could probably gently nudge them into returning it as well.

It was time for a little candle magick. I lifted my large cast-iron cauldron and set it on top of the wood-burning stove. I placed the candle inside the cauldron and went to sit on the couch to meditate for a moment and to think about who I should call on. Which deity would best help us find the missing flute? I closed my eyes, sat back, and let myself drift for a while.

The image of the Hindu god Krishna came to my mind, which, I will admit, surprised me somewhat. My eyes opened on a chuckle. Krishna? I have never really been into the Hindu gods. I was familiar with the god Shiva, he is sometimes called the Lord of the Dance or the God of Change. Then there is Kali the Crone, who protects women from violence, but I had never worked with or researched Krishna. The only thing I remembered was that he was blue, associated with love and music, and often portrayed playing the flute.

I closed my eyes again and concentrated on Krishna's image. A warm, happy feeling came over me and I opened my eyes, confident in my visualization. Krishna it was, then. I blew out a breath, walked over to the cauldron, and cast a quick circle. In this case, casting a circle seemed appropriate, since I was working some rather intense magick. I felt that by casting a circle it would help to reinforce my spell. I only wanted to nudge someone into telling us where the flute was, to prick their conscience, nothing more.

I asked the Goddess to guide me and to keep the magick nonmanipulative. I then improvised a sincere, quick prayer to Krishna and asked for his help in finding my daughter's flute, today. I also asked the Goddess for justice and for my daughter's sadness to be alleviated, as she was very upset by the whole situation. I lit the candle, intoned a candle charm over it, and left it to burn merrily inside the cauldron. Then I closed up the spell and threw some towels into the washing machine.

About an hour and a half later, the phone rang. It was the school's DARE police officer. He was very excited. They had a lead on the flute. Within the last hour, a student had stepped forward with information and someone else had, well, spilled the beans. Could I meet him at a pawnshop in ten minutes to identify what they suspected was my daughter's flute?

A detective from the police department met us there, and the detective went in first. He asked me if I would be able to identify the flute case and I told him that I could easily, as Kat had put blue moon and gold star stickers on the case. He nodded and told me to wait. After about fifteen minutes of sitting in my car, I was climbing the walls. So I got out and walked over to the police car to talk to the DARE officer. Here I was, on my day off, hanging out with a couple of police officers outside of a pawnshop, all because of that spell.

While we waited for the detective to come out of the pawnshop, my cell phone rang.

I checked my watch; high school was out. I bet my sons wondered where I was.

"Mom?" It was my middle son. "What's up with the big spell candle? Where are you?"

"Hanging out with the police," I answered blandly, as the police radio squawked loudly behind me.

"Geez, Mom!" He started to laugh. "Do I want to know why?"

"They think your sister's flute was taken to a pawnshop," I answered him. "I'll call you back when I know something."

The good news was that it *was* her flute. The kids hadn't managed to peel off all of the moon and star stickers on the case. I had a few things to say to the owner of the pawnshop, and what I didn't think to say, the nice detective did. The flute was taken to the police station as evidence. Seems they had been trying to nail this pawnshop for some time. It must have been an exciting day for the DARE officer. He got to interrogate a couple of kids, identify stolen goods, and assist a detective in catching a pawnshop that was buying stolen merchandise from minors.

On a happy note, the detective and the DARE officer managed to get the flute returned to my daughter by the end of the day. I had to fill out some forms and they wanted to photograph the flute, and then we could pick it up from the police station later in the evening. The DARE officer had a big smile on his face when he handed the flute back to my daughter, and asked her to play it for him. Kat slid the flute together and played a quick scale. The flute was in good shape, and the detective and the DARE officer commented on how incredibly lucky we were.

Then the detective added, "Isn't it great when things fall into place, like they are supposed to?"

"Yeah," I agreed with a smile, "it's just like magick."

My daughter only elbowed me slightly in the ribs for that comment.

Natural Magick Quickies for Emergencies

Here are some quick, creative ideas for natural magick when you are faced with an emergency. Don't panic. Stop, ground, and center. Ask the God and Goddess to guide you. Think about your options for a moment, and then come up with a bold, magickal plan of action.

Tempest in a Tealight

Try a little fire magick. Light a plain tealight candle and ask the God and Goddess for their help. Try using this all-purpose candle charm:

> *Little white candle burning so bright,*
>
> *I call upon the powers of magick this night.*
>
> *Lord and Lady, help me in my time of need,*
>
> *grant my request with all possible speed.*

(Pause here and briefly state the problem or your request for assistance.) Close the spell with,

In no way will this spell reverse,

or place upon me any curse.

Allow the tealight to burn out in a safe place. Now think about all of those correspondences in the other chapters for flowers, foliage, and crystals. What do you suppose you could add to that little tealight spell for a specific purpose, or to personalize it? You may add one or all of these goodies to your spell:

Prosperity: Maple leaf, honeysuckle flowers, a malachite or aventurine stone.

Healing: A red carnation, a pot of blooming hyacinths, marigolds, a bloodstone, a carnelian, and some spring water (you can use bottled).

Protection: Elm leaf, an oak leaf, a moonstone, and tiger's-eye.

Friendship: Zinnia, pine needles, an amethyst, and rose quartz.

Spice Rack Sorcery

Did you know that many of the spices you cook with have magickal properties and uses? No kidding. You can use cinnamon to promote prosperity and to encourage happy vibrations. Garlic powder helps to dissolve angry feelings and clear the air after an argument. Salt is a purifier and also banishes negativity. And those are just a few examples. Let me give you a quick list with ideas on how to use these spices for a little kitchen Witch magick.

Chives: Removes pessimistic feelings.

Cinnamon: Prosperity, security, and love.

Cloves: Protection, safety, and stopping gossip.

Dill: Protection and prosperity.

Fennel: Health and purification.

Garlic: Dissolves angry, hurt feelings and is protective.

Rosemary: Remembrance, love, and health.

Sage: Wisdom.

Salt: Cleanses and removes negativity.

Thyme: New projects.

You can sprinkle a little of these spices and herbs on an unlit candle or take a four-by-four-inch square of fabric and put the loose spices into the center. You could add a coordinating stone or crystal to add a little oomph to the magick. Draw up the edges and tie the little bundle closed with a ribbon.

Spicy Charm Bag Ideas

Keep your charm bags small. Use either plain, inexpensive cotton fabric such as muslin, or colored fabrics that you can match up to your magickal purpose. If you use plain white muslin, then tie the bag shut with a colored ribbon to employ a little color magick into your charm bag. Watch for sales and check out the bargain tables at the fabric store. A quarter of a yard of fabric won't cost much, and it will make several charm bags. Here are some quick recipes for charm bags. These can be made with a tumbling stone or two and the herbs and spices typically found in the kitchen cupboard.

Protection: Salt, a clove of garlic, and a cinnamon stick. Add an obsidian for protection or a quartz crystal for more power. Tie it closed with a red ribbon.

Romantic Vibrations: A cinnamon stick, a tablespoon of salt, and a tablespoon of rosemary. Add a rose quartz for loving vibrations and a moonstone for empathy. Fasten the bag closed with a pink ribbon.

Prosperity: A cinnamon stick, a tablespoon of dill, and three new shiny dimes. Add an aventurine stone for prosperity and a malachite to bring cash. Knot the bag closed with a green or a gold ribbon.

Safe Driver: A clove of garlic to dispel road rage, a tablespoon of salt to banish negativity, and a tablespoon of dill for protection. Add one obsidian stone for protection and a tiger's-eye tumbling stone. Secure the bag with a red, a white, and a black ribbon. These colors represent the Triple Goddess.

When you have created the charm bag you may set it next to a spell candle, or place the bag somewhere inconspicuous in the room where an argument took place, or carry it with you. To avoid misunderstandings and problems, I do not recommend taking a spice or herb-filled charm bag to school or leaving it in your school locker, as it could be mistaken for an illegal substance. If you keep a charm bag in your car, make sure that the spices you use are easily identified and recognizable as cooking spices.

I made up a tiny spice-filled charm bag for my oldest son to keep in the family car's glove box. I used some red-colored fabric for protection, and then tied it up with a white ribbon for peace. The purpose of the charm bag was to keep the older car running smoothly and to keep him safe from harm. In the bag was an obsidian stone for protection, salt to reduce negativity, a cinnamon stick for security, and a garlic clove for more protection. Lastly, I added a fresh sage leaf from the garden for wisdom (I wanted him to be both a smart and a safe driver). Did the charm bag work? Yes, it did.

A few days before school started this past summer, my son was out running some errands in the family car—you know, depositing his paycheck and getting a haircut, that sort of thing. He was minding his own business and yielding to oncoming traffic when another driver, going at least thirty to thirty-five miles an hour, plowed into him. Both our car and the other driver's car were totaled. The other driver hit him so hard it knocked his contacts out and knocked him for a loop.

He staggered out of the car, asked the other driver if they were okay, and then climbed over an embankment to go into a shop across the road for help. (He had forgotten to take his cell phone along.) Some men from a nearby shop grabbed him and made him sit down. My son called home, and then they called 911. I don't think I will ever forget the few moments that it took us to drive across town to find him, praying to the God and Goddess the whole way, not knowing exactly where he was or how badly he was hurt. That's not something I ever care to re-live.

When we arrived, the firefighters and paramedics were checking my son out as he leaned his six-foot-four frame against the guardrail. I pulled up behind a police car and my husband and I jumped out and ran to get to him. What terrified me was the condition of the other driver's car. The front end was pretty much gone and there was broken glass and twisted parts of cars all over the road. The only way I could get to my son quickly was to go between what was left of the two cars. I recall vaguely the paramedics were open-mouthed and gesturing about going a different way as I ran to him. At the moment, I could have cared less.

I had to check myself to keep from grabbing him. He was very pale but standing up, so I knew his injuries weren't life-threatening. So I settled for a one-armed sort of hug. Laying my head on his chest, I tearfully asked him if he knew how badly he was hurt. Could he move his arms and legs? He raised his hands in the air, weakly shook them, and then raised an eyebrow at me—a tough guy to hysterical mother kind of thing. I laughed and backed out of the way to let the paramedics do their job.

My husband walked quietly up to our son and asked him if he was okay. Then he calmly went over to the police officer and asked him some questions about the accident. A few moments later they asked my husband if he could pull our car off the street, since it was blocking traffic. Our car was sort-of driveable, but the back bumper was a memory. They had to call a tow truck to move the other car.

As my husband slowly eased our car out of the way, I asked the police officer if the other driver was all right. The accident had been their fault and the other driver was even ticketed at the scene. He told me yes, and that they were very sorry. I turned to focus on the other driver. I didn't say a word but I guess there must have been something in my expression or in my body language because I found myself caught firmly in a bear hug from the police officer. He softened his restraint with a couple of pats on the back. I immediately sensed what he was doing, so I relaxed and told him that I would behave. *Harm none,* I reminded myself. That includes regular life as well, not just magick.

Then the police officer let me go, but he held my hand. (Guess he didn't trust me.) At that point, a paramedic and another officer asked me if they could see my feet. I looked at them both incredulously, ignored their request, and told them to worry about my son. Finally, one of the paramedics just knelt down by me and said, "Okay, ma'am, let's take a look here." Then he firmly nabbed my ankle to inspect my feet.

"What are you looking for?" I asked him.

He was looking for cuts. When we had first arrived at the accident, I had run straight through the broken metal, plastic, and glass with open sandals on. To his amazement, my feet were fine, I didn't even have a scratch.

My son got a trip to the emergency room in the ambulance on a backboard and in a neck brace. Since he had a very sore neck and a walloping headache, they didn't want to take any chances. I rode along in the front seat of the ambulance and my husband followed us in our other car. The paramedics complimented my son's behavior and cool thinking after the accident. Sure, he was a little goofy from getting hit so hard, but he had checked the other driver to see if they were all right and then went for help. After some x-rays that turned out to be clear and some pain medication, they sent my son home from the ER with instructions to follow up with his doctor. Whiplash was the diagnosis, and it is a very real thing.

He ended up doing several months of physical therapy for his neck and back injuries. But, when all was said and done, he walked away from the accident. It is humbling to realize how much worse it could have been. That old, reliable car was history, but my son was okay. I'll trade a car for my child any day of the week.

So do my son and I believe that the little charm bag worked? Absolutely.

Kat's Freezer Bag Magick

Another spin on charm bags is a popular Witch's trick for putting the big chill on a nasty, spiteful person or hurtful situation. Sometimes this is called freezer magick. Typically, you use a small resealable sandwich bag and a half-cup of water. In this bag you add a pinch of salt to dissolve negativity and a coordinating witchy spice or herb, depending on the situation. (See the chart on pages 211–212 for magickal spices.)

If the situation involves another person, then you add to the bag a sample of their handwriting—their signature, if you can get it. This handwriting sample represents this person and it ties this "calm down and cool off" magick firmly to them. This type of magick is not manipulative, as long as your intentions are only to let things cool off and settle down for a time so you can deal with the situation calmly. When things have settled down, take the sandwich bag out of the freezer and let it melt. Then toss the bag and its contents in the trash and put the whole thing behind you.

When would this type of magick be appropriate? I have used this type of freezer magick to stop gossip, to calm down an old family argument, and to make someone stop harassing me at my job. I kept that "job" bag in the freezer for almost three months. Finally, the problematic coworker was reprimanded, written up, and transferred. After they were gone, I chucked the freezer bag. Good riddance.

Remember to try all mundane actions first. See if you can resolve the situation by talking to the other person or people involved. If that doesn't work, then your next step would be asking for help. Try your parents first. After all, they love you and they will want to help you out if they can. If this is a situation at school, then go to your counselor or to a peer helper or conflict mediator. Try talking to a teacher that you trust. If it is a conflict at your job, go to your supervisor right away and report it, or ask for their help. If you get stuck in the middle of feuding friends, you have two choices: either try and mediate, or get out of the line of fire.

Little melodramas like this happen all the time when you are a teen. Hey, they happen when you are an adult, too. However, I will not insult you by saying that it is not a big deal and to just go make a new friend. To the people involved, it is a big deal, and getting stuck in the middle can really hurt your feelings. When this type of situation happened to my daughter, she decided to take matters into her own hands and put the freeze on this nasty little situation.

My daughter and two of her classmates had all been best friends for a long time. When the other two friends began to fight, Kat found herself in the middle of the quarrel, and she refused to take sides. The next thing she knew, one friend was spreading some nasty gossip and whispering behind her back, and the other wouldn't even talk to my daughter anymore—all because Kat didn't take sides in their fight.

Unbeknownst to me, Kat quietly gathered handwriting samples from each of her two pals. (This wasn't difficult for Kat to get, as there had been a major shuffling back and forth of nasty notes as the situation escalated.) Kat cut out their signatures and some really hateful lines from the notes. Then Kat took two resealable sandwich bags and put these samples into separate bags, one bag for each person.

Into these bags, she added a half-cup of water, and sprinkled in some salt for its cleansing properties. Next she added a pinch of garlic powder to break up the hateful vibes and bad feelings. To the gossiper's bag she added a teaspoon of cloves to help stop the rumors that they had been spreading. Kat then sealed up the sandwich bags and chucked them into the freezer. She closed the door firmly and told them both to cool off and to stop all their nastiness, *now*.

The next day, neither of the two individuals looked at or spoke to Kat. Kat took this as an improvement, as it certainly beat the gossiping and whispering. A few days later, one friend began talking to her again and told her that they were sorry for ever dragging her into the middle of the argument. The gossiper, on the other hand, left Kat completely alone, and they were never really close friends again. They are polite to each other and they get along well enough, they just don't hang out together anymore.

At the time, I was unaware of the magick Kat had performed. I thought she might be up to something—she definitely had a magickal vibe to her—but she never said a word. The only reason I even found out about it was quite by accident. It was about a week or so after the incident and my husband was rearranging the freezer to make more room for groceries. As he shuffled things around, two ice-filled sandwich bags fell out of the freezer and onto the kitchen floor.

"Honey," he called me into the kitchen.

"Yeah?" I answered, as I poked my head around the corner.

He held up the two bags and asked me, "Is somebody giving you a hard time at work again?"

"No, why do you ask? " I said, as he showed me the bags. I took the bags from him and looked them over. "These aren't mine."

We looked at each other for a moment and then, in unison, called our daughter into the kitchen. "Kat!"

All attitude, she strolled into the kitchen. "What?" she asked us.

"Tell me about these," I asked her as I tried to keep a straight face.

"Oh," she said as she blew her bangs out of her eyes, "that's from a few days ago. I'll let them thaw out eventually, when they stop acting like such jerks."

"Would I be correct in assuming that these represent your two bickering friends?" I said soberly.

"Yep," she said, hand on one hip.

"Did you use samples of their handwriting? Their signatures?" I asked her.

"I did." Now she was grinning. "Just like you taught me."

I tossed the sandwich bags back into the freezer and closed the door. "So, how's it working?" I asked, as my husband crossed the room to answer the ringing telephone.

"Kat," he spoke up. "You've got a phone call."

She waltzed over and took the cordless phone from her father. It was one of the friends in question, calling to apologize. Kat tossed me a superior smirk, and then went into her room to take her phone call in private.

"Well," I said with a laugh to my husband. "I guess the spell is working out just fine."

TWELVE

A Natural Witch

A natural Witch may be described as someone who follows a path of magick intuitively, for their magickal talent comes from within. They can be solitary Witches (they practice alone) or they may work magick with a group of close friends. They could even be a member of a formal circle or a coven.

A natural Witch arrives into this world with their senses already sharpened. They may be naturally psychic or empathic. These intuitive people are the ones who are aware of the energies and magick of nature that are all around them. As they mature, they become aware that there seems to be more to this old world than what they ever possibly imagined. And so they begin their search for answers.

Someone said to me, quite recently, that they were surprised to find out that I was a Witch, because I seemed too normal to them. After all, they explained, I had a full-time job, I am married, and I have three normal teenagers. They explained their comment by telling me that I seemed "too down-to-earth and practical to be someone who still believed in things like magic and casting spells."

I thanked them for the compliment and then explained my certainty in magick this way. An individual's belief in whether or not magick is real depends on their perception level. The certainty that magick is, indeed, real has a lot to do with how intuitive and sensitive you are. My theory is that some people can sense this energy and others cannot.

This may happen for a couple of reasons. One, they may be too afraid and close-minded. Or, two, they may be so wrapped up in the rat race and their pursuit of material things that they couldn't even imagine that such a beautifully simple and natural thing like magick could possibly be true.

To be a natural Witch means that you are following your instincts. You listen to your heart and to your head, and then you go where the magick of life takes you. By studying natural magick, you have started down a fascinating road. This is but one of many magickal paths that awaits you.

The Witch's Pyramid

So, what do you think so far, Teen Witch? Are you ready to expand your mind a little further? You and I have been covering the techniques of natural magick and Witchcraft throughout this book, and we have discussed many earthy and magickal topics.

Now I want to give you some more of the philosophy behind the tradition of Witchcraft. You are already familiar with the law of three—this being what you send out, you will receive in turn, times three—and the Wiccan Rede, "An' it harm none, do what you will." Think you're ready for some more lessons? Here's a good one. Have you ever heard of the Witch's pyramid?

The Witch's pyramid is the following statement: "To know, to dare, to will, and to be silent." And it is so much more than a clever line that you rattle off to impress your friends. These ten little words may be looked on as the building blocks of magick. When you understand the meanings behind these words, you begin to comprehend how magick works and why this idea of the Witch's pyramid is so important.

To Know

"To know" means to know yourself—who you are and what you're about. Flip back to the end of chapter 2, where there are journal pages. See where I asked you for your thoughts on what you imagined made for a good and ethical Witch? What was your answer? If you had to rewrite your answer now, what would it be? Now, how much more have you learned since you've been trying your hand at natural magick? If you have worked your way through the book to this point, then you get the whole "knowledge" thing. You are and have been seeking knowledge and discovering different aspects of yourself.

This is an important step forward for you. The words "to know" mean that you are taking a good, honest look at yourself and what you want out of life. The new information that you are learning can be applied to all aspects of your life, school, and family, even your job and friends. Whether you realize it or not, you have grown and expanded your mind since you began reading this book. Now it's up to you as to what you decide to do with this knowledge.

To Dare

"To dare" means that you are daring to study and practice natural magick techniques on your own. This can be a tough one. It's not like there is a Witch hotline or anything . . . Sometimes there isn't anyone to ask when you have a question or are unsure of what to do next. You have to be smart and determined to figure a lot of magick out for yourself. The most talented and, yes, powerful Witches that I know read and study and then decide for themselves how magick works for them. They dare to practice and learn on their own. Just as we discussed in the last chapter, they may make mistakes from time to time, but they also learn from them. They are wise and talented individuals, as are you.

The word "dare" may be defined as being sufficiently courageous—to have sufficient courage and to perform an action as proof of your courage. It also means "to confront boldly." Well, are we feeling bold and courageous? You bet you are. Anybody who has the guts and determination to discover the truth about magick and Witchcraft is courageous. You have tossed away lies and misinformation and looked into the shining face of the truth. Witchcraft and natural magick are indeed bold and beautiful things. Hold your head up and be proud of who you are! Walking the path of the Witch is a brave and daring thing to do. Be confident in your choices, for you are daring to be wise.

To Will

The word "will" is defined as a desire or a wish. It means to express determination and persistence. "To will" is to will positive changes in your life with your magick. These mental personal powers can manifest themselves as magick. By using the natural magick techniques that you have studied in this book, you should have an idea of how to go about doing just that. Way back in the beginning chapters we talked about personal power and how to focus your positive intentions. I am going to remind you of these philosophies once again.

Harm none, not even yourself, through your magick. Be kind and loving in your everyday life as well as your magickal one. If it is your desire to bring about a better life for yourself, then you can start this process by showing kindness to others. Have the will, determination, and strength to live your life as a caring and ethical person, and a wise Witch.

To Be Silent

The phrase "to be silent" is pretty self-explanatory. To be silent is, in truth, the foundation that the other principles are built on, and often the hardest to achieve. Silence is often referred to as the secret to keeping secrets. Basically what this means is that if you perform a spell, don't go off flapping your gums about it. What, are you looking to brag or something? Yapping about your magick to other people only gets you in trouble. They will either think that you are a showoff or they will think that you have a desperate need for attention.

There is an old saying in the Craft that goes like this, "Do a spell and then forget about it." What this means is work your magick and then believe in it. In other words, that you *know* it will work because you *dared* to have the *will* to make the positive change. Be strong and quiet about your spellwork. Watch and wait to see how it unfolds. Nervously confiding in your buddies that you did a spell to pass your history test will only cause disbelief—which is a negative emotion that you don't need—and it may hamper the spell's success.

Or you may find yourself in the middle of a well-meaning but unnecessary debate about religion. That whole "my religion is real and yours is not" argument can be a nasty one. Do you want to have to calm Mary Jane down as she launches into a top-volume pilgrimage over the lunch table? I didn't think so.

When and if you decide to share your beliefs with other people, including your family, is up to you. Think carefully about it and plan ahead. Don't just drop a bombshell on them. That's not the way to convince them that everything is okay. I really wish that I could sit here and tell you that if you plan to announce over the dinner table that you are studying Witchcraft, then your family won't even blink an eye . . . but that just is not true.

"Mom, Dad," you'd make this imagined announcement as dinner is being served, "I'm studying Witchcraft."

"That's lovely, dear." In your fantasy, your mother smiles at you. "Please pass the potatoes."

This, unfortunately, is not the way real life works. I have met plenty of young people who have had their parents stumble across their magickal books and then destroy them. They don't read them, they don't discuss the books with their children, they only panic and then react out of ignorance and fear.

One young lady I met was a college student who lived in the dorms at school. She kept her magickal books hidden in the trunk of her car when she came home for the summer. The reason for all of the drama? Well, her mother had found a book on the Craft in her room a year or two earlier, and tore the girl's room to shreds, even the mattress. (The woman sounds a little psycho to me.) The girl's mother burned the book and called in a minister. When the young lady arrived home from school that afternoon, she had one hell of a messy situation on her hands, including purchasing a new mattress—a worst-case scenario if I ever heard one.

Did the girl give up magick? No, she did not. Instead, she went underground and practiced very quietly. She switched to using natural representations only, like a pebble or a flower, and hid any and all books and other magickal supplies so her mother could not destroy her property again.

At the opposite end of the spectrum, I also know a young man who was very curious about Witchcraft, so I recommended that he read a popular title about the Craft that was specifically written for teens. He worked through the book and then shared it with his mother. Bless her heart, she not only studied the book but checked the suggested reading list at the end of it as well. She even went to the bookstore with him to help him choose some more good titles for him to read.

I next saw him on Halloween, walking with his friends. He had on a long, dark blue velvet robe that his mother had made for him. When he turned around to show me the back, he proudly announced that the silver pentagram that was embroidered there was done by his mom. And what do you know? She decided that she was interested in magick as well. As the family had an Asian heritage, his mom had become fascinated with Kwan Yin. She wanted him to ask me where she could find more information about her. There is a true best-case scenario.

Probably you will fall somewhere in the middle of these. If you are fortunate, you will have open-minded parents and you can discuss your interest in magick and the Craft with them. Listen to their opinions and share your reading material. Follow the house rules and, if they are totally against the subject and ban any reading material, then you are going to have to be patient and abide by their wishes. Natural magick isn't going anywhere. It's been around for thousands of years and it will still be waiting for you when you get older and move out on your own.

If this is the case, then I suggest you use the techniques that were presented in this book and celebrate your connection to the natural world quietly. The magickal powers of nature are all around you. Get outside and see what you can learn from looking at the world with a Witch's eyes.

Keep the lines of communication open between yourself and your folks. Then just go about being who you are. Proving to them that you are indeed all right, keeping up your grades, and just being a normal kid will go a long way toward relieving some of their fears. Have a quiet faith in yourself and your abilities. Dare to believe in yourself and have the will and desire to change your life for the better.

Teen Witch Test

Well, let's see how much you have learned so far. Take this fun little Teen Witch Test, and no peeking for the answers. Here is where your sense of honor comes into play. Don't panic, now, this is for fun and to show you how much new knowledge you really have acquired. Answer the questions and then, when you are finished, grade yourself. And yes, all of the answers to these questions can be found within this book.

1. List the four directions and their coordinating elements, colors, and tools.

2. What is the rule of three? Explain this please.

3. What is the Wiccan Rede?

4. Explain, briefly, what "grounding and centering" is.

5. Finish this sentence. "Magick is the art and science of . . ."

6. List two possible definitions for the word *Wicca*.

7. What is magickal herbalism?

8. What natural item may you use as a substitute for a candle in a spell?

9. What is an elemental?

10. List the four nature spirits that were discussed in this book and their elemental correspondences.

11. Who is the Green Man?

12. What are the three faces of the Goddess?

13. List the eight sabbats and their dates.

14. Rose petals are used for what purpose in a spell?

15. What is a pentagram? What does it stand for?

16. Before casting a spell for another person, what is the first thing that you should do?

17. Match up the candle color to the magickal purpose.

Red	friendship
Orange	removing negativity
Yellow	all-purpose
Green	love and protection
Blue	knowledge
Purple	energy and vitality
Black	prosperity and garden magick
White	peace and healing
Pink	power and faerie magick

18. Why do you want to become a Witch?

19. What is the Witch's pyramid?

20. What are the most important tools that every Witch owns?

Well, how did you do? If you found that you missed a lot of questions or that you were unsure of the answers, then go back and reread the book. You may try taking notes or using a bright yellow pen to highlight certain things (I do that all of the time). If you are sure of yourself and comfortable with your answers, then you may want to go on to the next step in your journey: a dedication ritual.

The Dedicant and a Year and a Day

Performing a dedication is a way to get your feet wet in the Craft. A dedication ritual is a method of introducing yourself to the God and the Goddess. You are formally declaring your interest in natural magick and that you would like them to watch over you and to guide you for the next year. For most traditional Witches, this dedicant phase lasts for a year and a day. After a person undergoes a dedication, they are expected to study and practice and learn over the course of a full calendar year. This gives them a chance to tune into the rhythms of the solar year and an opportunity to celebrate all of the sabbats and full moons over a twelve-month period of time.

During this period, you get to decide whether or not the Craft is right for you. You may decide after a year that maybe this isn't for you after all. And that's fine. If you work your way through the year, quietly celebrating the sabbats and enjoying the full moons, and you are still fascinated by the whole idea, then you will probably continue on with your studies.

Why is the time phase so long? Well, "Instant Witches" are everywhere these days. They play around with a spell or two, skim through a book, or get inspired by a television character, and declare that they too are a "witch." And they are not too hard to spot. These dabblers are usually flitting around trying to look gothic and mysterious. When you encounter one, don't get angry—just smile and ask them if they had a nice Mabon, and watch them look at you in confusion.

If you've learned anything about magick by now, it should be that you have to work for it. Real Witches never stop studying and learning. The skills and techniques of natural magick are not difficult to learn, but you still have to practice to become proficient at them. The truth is, it does take time.

Instead of grumbling about it or whining (*What do you mean, a whole year?*), use this time wisely and discover for yourself the natural magick of the four seasons. See what lessons you learn from observing the sabbats. Start a journal and keep notes on what different energies the various seasons of the year have to offer you. You may find that you feel energized and have lots of creative energy in the spring. The summer months may cause you to feel mellow, laid back, and more open to new ideas. The fall months may bring about a new awareness of magick and the spiritual planes, while the winter months may make you yearn to snuggle in and study.

This twelve-month period of time should be looked on as a gift, for that is exactly what it is. Get out there and open your heart and mind to all of the magickal energies of nature. Experience all of the beauty of the four bewitching seasons. If you feel that you are whole-heartedly ready to begin this new phase of your journey, then read over the ceremony below and decide for yourself if this is what you want to do.

A Dedication Ceremony

You may wish to choose ahead of time a piece of magickal jewelry to symbolize your dedication. Jewelry made of silver is more affordable and it is also the metal that is associated with the moon, magick, and the Goddess. Here are a few suggestions for an attractive and subtle dedication piece. Celtic knotwork is always a popular choice. A silver ring that is set with a crystal or semiprecious stone is another idea. Or you could look for a pretty moonstone pendant that is set in silver. How about an attractive crystal point, like an amethyst or a clear quartz crystal, that you can slip onto a chain? You could try a crescent moon, a star pendant, or a silver charm. Use your imagination and see what you can find.

An opportune time to perform your dedication ritual is on a night of a full moon. The full moon is a time of increased psychic awareness and magickal powers. You may choose to work outside in your sacred space or, if the weather does not permit, then set up in a private place indoors. If possible, choose a spot that will give you a view of the moon.

Take a bath and wear fresh, clean clothes. Set up your work area and gather your supplies. Back in chapter 9 we went over altars and sacred indoor spaces, so if you are indoors, refer to those instructions. If you choose to head outdoors, then you'll need to take along some magickal supplies. These supplies may include a cup or chalice full of spring water, illuminator candles (try those glass globe citronella candles, they will keep away mosquitoes and the flames will be protected from the breeze), a natural representation of each of the four elements, and a portrayal of the God and Goddess. For the God, you may use an oak leaf or acorns; for the Goddess, try a white rose or other flower.

If you have created any magickal tools, bring these along as well. Set up your work surface so it is attractive and festive. Set your dedication jewelry on the work surface between your candles. If you have a pentacle, place the jewelry on the pentacle.

I. CAST THE CIRCLE

(A circle is appropriate in this case, as a dedication ritual is a formal event.) Begin in the north and turn to the right. Walk the boundary of the circle and say the following:

I cast this dedication circle by the powers

of earth, air, fire, and water.

(start in the north) *Earth brings me strength.*

(move to the east) *Air grants me knowledge.*

(walk to the south) *Fire bestows protection.*

(finish in the west) *Water blesses me with love.*

(move to the center) *As above, so below.*

The elemental powers spin and my magick holds.

The circle is sealed.

II. STATEMENT OF PURPOSE AND BLESSING

Move to the center of the circle. Hold your hands out to your sides, palms up, and tip your face up to the light of the full moon. Then say:

There are many paths to divinity and each must choose his or her own.

This is the path that I choose. I call on the God and the Goddess.

Here, in the circle, I open my heart and ask for your blessing.

I ask for your loving guidance and protection over the next full year.

Dip your fingers into the water and, with your wet fingers, draw a pentacle on your forehead and over your heart. Then continue by saying:

Your voices speak inside of me, as they do in all of nature's creatures,

if we will only stop and listen. Help me to listen and to learn.

Teach me that magick is to be found in both the heart and the mind.

Assist me as I continue to grow in beauty and strength,

and joy and wisdom. So mote it be!

III. THE OATH

Lower your hands and center yourself. When you feel ready, then continue by saying,

> *I, _____, do of my own free will and mind*
> *promise to abide by the laws of natural magick*
> *and the tradition of the Craft.*
> *I will commemorate the sabbats and celebrate the full moons.*
> *I pledge to harm none with my magick and I will abide by the rule of three.*
> *I will keep my promise to study and learn for a full year.*
> *On my honor, I swear this oath. Blessed be.*

Pick up the jewelry and let the light of the moon shine down on it for a moment. Sprinkle a little of the water on it. Then say:

> *May this jewelry be a symbol of my dedication and my connection*
> *to the God and Goddess. May I wear it proudly.*

Slip the jewelry on.

IV. CLOSING

Take a sip of the water and pour the rest onto the ground for the God and Goddess. (If you are indoors, wait until you are finished and then pour the water into a flowerpot or onto the grass outside.)

Thank the God and Goddess for their time and attention. Say:

> *I thank the God and Goddess for their time and care.*
> *I close this ceremony now by the powers of earth, water, fire, and air.*

Open up the circle by starting in the west. Say:

> *Thank you, element of water. Continue to bless me*
> *with love and compassion during the approaching year.*

Turn to the left. Walk to the south and declare:

Thank you, element of fire. Keep the flame of courage
burning bright within me during the next year.

Turn to your left and go to the east. Now state:

Thank you, element of air. Continue to grant me knowledge
and inspiration in the coming year.

Finally, turn to the left again, and return to the direction north.

Thank you, element of earth. Help me to remain strong and true
during this forthcoming year.

Move to the center of the circle. Then announce:

The circle is open but unbroken,
merry meet, merry part and merry meet again.

V. GROUND AND CENTER

Sink down to the ground for a moment and center yourself. Take a few stabilizing breaths and draw up revitalizing energy from the Earth. When you feel that you have finished, then stand up and brush off your hands.

Extinguish the candles, and clean up your area. Put away any supplies and go have a snack. Congratulations, dedicant!

Wicca 101

So where do you go from here? You go on to the next part of your journey. This next year is your personal time to follow where your curiosity leads you. Study and decide for yourself what your magickal specialties are, and what area of magick you'd like to focus on.

For starters, I would go back over this book again and make some notes on the suggested reading material that was at the end of several of the chapters. Try the library first and see what they have available. If you decide to take a trip to the bookstore, keep a good grip on your cash and be smart. The sheer number of titles in the New Age/Occult sections can be overwhelming. Pick up a few that catch your eye and thumb through them.

If they don't feel right or you find yourself rolling your eyes over them, then put them back. Here are a few hints to help you find a keeper.

- Look to see if the book has a bibliography. This usually tells you that the author did their homework and researched the topic.

- Ask a friendly employee at the store if they can recommend a magickal title, or ask what their biggest sellers are.

- Check a few Pagan/Wiccan online sites and see if they have book reviews. Read the book review and decide for yourself.

Here is a short list of some of my favorites, with my comments on the books. Thumb through these and check them out for yourself, for further study. Remember what I said—a Witch never stops studying and learning.

WITCHCRAFT/WICCA

Teen Witch: Wicca for a New Generation by Silver Ravenwolf. (A groundbreaker. This book paved the way for the many teen books that followed. Detailed and crammed full of information on traditional Witchcraft.)

Spells for Teenage Witches by Marina Baker. (This book has a British flavor, as the author is English. A few British slang words may throw you, but you can figure them out quickly enough. For example, we call 'em zits and they call them spots. However, it is a light, fun, and sassy book. It is also beautifully illustrated.)

To Ride a Silver Broomstick by Silver Ravenwolf. (One of my all-time favorites, a solid Wicca 101 book. This book is great for anybody, no matter what their age.)

The Complete Idiot's Guide to Wicca and Witchcraft by Denise Zimmer-
mann and Katherine A. Gleason. (Don't let the title put you off.
This is a fabulous book. I recommend this book all of the time to
newer Witches. It's humorous, nonthreatening, and easy to read.
It has tons of good, solid, and practical information.)

The Real Witches' Handbook by Kate West. (If you are curious about
how Witches do things over in the UK, then this is a fun and informative book, suitable for a beginner. You may find it interesting to
note the different names for the sabbats.)

MAGICKAL HERBALISM AND NATURAL MAGICK

Earth, Air, Fire, and Water: More Techniques of Natural Magic by Scott
Cunningham. (A fabulous book on natural magick, often referred
to as "standard issue" because most Witches have it.)

Garden Witchery: Magick from the Ground Up. by Ellen Dugan. (Yeah,
okay, it is my book. But if you liked chapter 7 of this book, then
you should enjoy my other one as well.)

FICTION

If you want something to read just for fun that has a witchy theme or a
magickal slant to it, try these titles.

Circle of Three series by Isobel Bird. (An enchanting, well-written series
about three teenage girls named Annie, Cooper, and Kate. The
books chronicle their initiatory year and the training and lessons
that the girls learn as they prepare to become full-fledged Witches
and members of a coven. To date, there are fifteen books in the
series. My daughter and I both read the entire series. We often
argued over who got to read the books first—they are *that* good.)

Sweep series by Cate Tiernan. (A fictional series of fourteen books
about a hereditary teenage Witch named Morgan. Drama, witchy
intrigue, and danger abound in this series. These books are a little
dramatic and dark, but good triumphs in the end. They are also a
lot of fun.)

The Mists of Avalon by Marion Zimmer Bradley. (The King Arthur
story as told from a woman's perspective. Full of Goddess and
Celtic mythology.)

The reading list given here and at the end of the other chapters
ought to keep you busy for awhile. Again, check out the library and see
what you can borrow. Also, while you're there, check for titles on the
Goddess, the Celts, and world mythology. If I can find magickal titles at
my hometown library, then I know you can. Just imagine—you, hanging out at the library, expanding your mind. Your parents will be
thrilled.

Teen Witches and the Future

To be a teen means that you are standing between two worlds: the
world of childhood and the world of adulthood. This in-between time
is full of adventure and discovery. It is also a time of trying out new
ideas and deciding for yourself what you would like to do with your
life. You have your whole life ahead of you and there are many paths to
choose from.

It is up to you to learn from as many different sources as you can.
And I'm not speaking of only magick. Knowledge is, indeed, power.
Continue your education. Listen and learn from your parents and from
your teachers. Pursue any and all opportunities for education and practical career training. Check the adult education classes at your community college and sign up for a few interesting classes over the summer.
See what opportunities present themselves. Expand your mind and
learn as much as you possibly can.

The Teen Witches of today are the future of the Craft. I want all of
you to be bright, successful, and talented individuals. Once you begin
to celebrate the energies of nature and tune into the quiet magick that
is always around you, your life will never be the same. Natural magick
changes you. It makes you more aware and more perceptive. It is my
hope that you will think about all of the lessons and ideas that were
presented in this book and apply them in a positive way to your life. I

remind my three teens all of the time that if they believe in themselves and are willing to work hard, anything is possible.

Do you think I am kidding? Just look at me. A few years ago, someone remarked to me that I could never become a writer. We both worked at a garden center for the summer and he was fresh out of college. He haughtily informed me that unless I had a degree in journalism, as he did, I was wasting my time pursuing my dreams. After all, what could a witchy mother of three and a gardener possibly offer to a professional publishing company? I thanked him for his advice and handed him a copy of the brand-new *Magical Almanac* for that year. (I had brought it along to work to show my friends.) In the almanac was my very first published article.

His mouth dropped open and he stammered out an apology. He read the article over carefully and asked where he could buy a copy. When I told him that the national chain bookstore at the mall would have them, his eyes went very wide. He congratulated me and walked away.

At the time, I was getting ready to begin my classes at a university to become certified as a Master Gardener. I took a lot of razzing about that at work. I was already a walking, talking font of information about gardening, and the nursery customers loved me. Why did I want to pursue this master gardening thing anyway? I took the Master Gardening classes so I could continue my education and because I wanted to learn more. It wasn't easy juggling two part-time jobs, a marriage, and three kids for a semester, but I did it.

When my classes were finished, I dove headfirst into volunteering in the community and teaching classes about gardening. I also began writing my very first book, *Garden Witchery,* and I guess the publishing company felt that I had plenty to offer after all, because they published it. Now if that's not magick, then I don't know what is.

Walking Your Path

Natural magick is truly to be found all around you. Take what you have discovered here and apply it to your life. Never stop studying and learning, and never give up your dreams! There is a whole wide and wonderful world out there for you to explore. So what are you waiting for?

I dare you: talk to the trees. Enjoy the warmth and magick of a campfire. Dip your feet in a lake and feel the breeze blow through your hair. Embrace all of the elements and all of the magickal wisdom that they can bring about. Tip up your face to the full moon and listen to what the Goddess has to say. Breathe in the wonder of the stars on a clear, frosty night. How much do you imagine they have seen? Acknowledge the might and life-giving warmth of the sun, and think of it as a symbol of the God and his love for the world.

Open your heart and mind to the beauty and magick of the natural world around you. You will not be disappointed. Go on, Teen Witch, make a believer out of me. Make your world a better place and practice your magick in an ethical way. Walk your chosen path wisely and enjoy your journey. Become a clever, loving, and wonderful Witch! You can truly do anything that you set your mind to.

Witches are wise and wonderful, this much is true.

If you believe in yourself, there is nothing you can't do.

For true magick does come from the heart and the mind.

May you hold these magickal lessons close, come rain or shine.

Blessed be!

Advanced practitioner: Comparable to a third-degree Witch. A practitioner with many years of experience. A high priest or high priestess.

Annual: A plant that completes its life cycle in one growing season.

Athame: A short, double-sided ritual knife. The athame is kept dull and never used to cut anything. (See chapter 9.)

Balefire: A small ritual fire, usually contained in a cauldron.

Banishing: Repelling an unwanted person or a bad situation.

Beltane: One of the greater sabbats, Beltane begins at sundown on April 30. May 1 is Beltane Day, also called May Day.

Blessed be: A greeting and a blessing exchanged by Pagans and Witches.

Bonfire: A large outdoor fire.

Brownies: A benevolent, industrious earth elemental. Brownies are considered to be earth spirits and house faeries.

Cauldron: A large kettle, typically iron, with three legs. A Witch's tool representing the element of water and a Goddess symbol of regeneration and rebirth. (See chapter 9.)

Charm: A rhyming series of words (a spell) used for a specific magickal purpose.

Circle mate: A friend and fellow member of a circle or a coven.

Clairvoyance: The psychic ability to "see" or sense people, places, and events from the past, present, or future.

Coven/Circle: A group of Wiccans that worship and study together.

the Craft: The Witches' name for the old religion and practice of Witchcraft.

Cunning man: An old term, traditionally meaning a male practitioner of the Arts.

Deosil: Moving in a clockwise direction, for casting circles and to bring forth positive influences.

Divination: The art and practice that seeks to foresee or foretell future events or hidden knowledge. Divination may be accomplished by psychic means or with the help of tarot cards, scrying, or runes.

Elementals: Spirits or energies that coordinate with each element. Earth elementals are brownies and gnomes. Air elementals are faeries and sylphs. Water elementals are mermaids, sirens, and undines. Fire elementals are the dragons.

Elements: Earth, air, fire, and water.

Empathy: A psychic ability in which a person may intuitively sense and experience other peoples' emotions and feelings.

Esbat: A coven/circle meeting or observance of a full moon.

Ethics: (If you don't know what these are, you are in *a lot* of trouble.) See chapter 2.

Faerie: A nature spirit. Usually an earth or air elemental.

Florigraphy: The language of flowers. See chapter 7.

Garden Witch: A practical, down-to-earth type of practitioner. A Witch who is well versed in herbal knowledge and its uses, and one who is a magickal gardener.

Green Man: A well-liked, traditional interpretation of the God. Also, the Green Man sculpture is enjoying a current level of popularity as a garden ornament. The Green Man ornament usually consists of a man's face surrounded by foliage and greenery.

Grounding and centering: A visualization technique. A way to focus and relax before or after performing magick. You push out negativity and stress from your own body. Then you pull back into your body healthy and strong energy from the Earth.

Herbalism: The use of herbs in conjunction with magick to bring about positive change.

Imbolc: A Wiccan sabbat. A cross-quarter day and one of four great sabbats. Traditionally celebrated on February 2. Also known as Brigid's day, Candlemas, and Groundhog Day. The first spring festival.

Intermediate practitioner: Comparable to a second-degree Witch, usually with three or more years of Craft experience under their belts.

Kitchen Witch: A hearth and home practitioner. One who celebrates and practices their craft in a quiet way using household spices, tools, and herbs.

Lammas/Lughnasadh: A greater sabbat that begins at sundown on July 31. Celebrated on August 1. The first of three harvest festivals.

Mabon: The autumnal equinox and a Wiccan sabbat. The Witches' Thanksgiving celebrated on or around September 21.

Magick: The combination of your own personal power used in harmony with natural objects such as crystals, herbs, and the elements. Magick is spelled with a "k" to denote the difference between a stage magician who pulls rabbits out of his hat and a *real* Witch's spell or natural magick.

Midsummer: The summer solstice and a Wiccan sabbat. Midsummer is celebrated on or around June 21. This sabbat is also known as Litha. An opportune time to communicate with the faeries.

Natural magician: A magician who works their magick mainly with the elements and in harmony with herbs and nature.

Novice: A beginner. A Witch with less than a year's experience.

Ostara: The vernal equinox and a Wiccan sabbat that falls on or around March 20. This is a spring celebration of the goddess Eostre, and is a time to rejoice in life and new beginnings.

Pentacle: The pentacle is a Witch's tool associated with the element of earth. It is a wooden or ceramic disc that has an upright five-pointed star surrounded by a circle in the center of the disc. Used as a power spot on a work area. You may charge jewelry, herbs, and charm bags on it.

Pentagram: A religious symbol for Witches. The Witch's pentagram is always upright and represents the four elements of earth, air, fire, and water. The topmost point of the star stands for the human spirit. The circle that surrounds the five-pointed star binds the magick together.

Perennial: A perennial plant is one that lives three or more years. Herbaceous perennials are plants that are nonwoody, and whose above-ground parts usually die to the ground each winter. They survive the winter by means of their vigorous root systems.

Sabbat: One of eight solar festivals or holidays celebrated by Pagan religions, including Imbolc, Ostara, Beltane, Midsummer, Lughnasadh, Mabon, Samhain, and Yule. Often divided up as greater and lesser sabbats. The greater sabbats are Imbolc, Beltane, Lughnasadh, and Samhain. The lesser sabbats, Ostara, Midsummer, Mabon, and Yule, fall on the equinoxes and the solstices. A fast way to distinguish between the greater and the lesser sabbats is to realize that the dates of the greater sabbats never change. The solstices and equinoxes shift from year to year, depending on when the sun moves into certain astrological signs.

Samhain: Also known as Halloween. The Witches' New Year. The day when the veil between our world and the spirit world is at its thinnest. This greater sabbat is celebrated on October 31. This popular holiday for children is also a time to honor the souls of loved ones who have passed, and a time to celebrate the coming year.

Staff: A magickal tool that represents the power to command and control magick. The staff is a walking stick crafted out of natural supplies. It represents the element of fire. (See chapter 9.)

Talisman: An object similar to an amulet that is designed for a specific magickal purpose.

Triple Moon Goddess: Refers to the three faces of the Goddess: the maiden, symbolized by the waxing moon; the mother, represented by the full moon; and the crone, who is in sympathy with the waning moon. One example of such a trinity would be Artemis, Selene, and Hecate. See chapter 8.

Wand: The wand is a tool of invocation. Typically made out of wood or metal, it represents the element of air. (See chapter 9.)

Wicca: The contemporary name for the religion of the Witch. Wicca takes its roots from the Anglo-Saxon word *wicce,* which may mean "wise." It is also thought to mean "to shape or bend." A Pagan religion based on the cycles of nature and the belief in karma, reincarnation, and the worship of both a God and a Goddess.

Wiccan Rede: The absolute rule that Witches and magicians live by. The Rede states simply, "Do as you will, harm none."

Widdershins: Working in a counterclockwise (banishing) direction.

Wisewomen: The first Witches and the custodians of the old herbal knowledge of benevolent spells and charms.

Witchcraft: The craft of the Witch.

Yule: The Wiccan sabbat celebrated on or around December 21. The winter solstice is the longest night and the shortest day. It is traditionally the time when Pagans celebrate the Mother Goddess and the return of the newly born Sun God. Decorated trees, the yule log, fresh holly, mistletoe, and evergreen wreaths feature prominently in our decorations.

Adams, Anton, and Mina Adams. *The Learned Art of Witches and Wizards.* Barnes and Noble Books, 2000.

Andrews, Ted. *Animal Speak.* St. Paul, Minn.: Llewellyn, 1994.

———. *Enchantment of the Faerie Realm.* St. Paul, Minn.: Llewellyn, 1993.

Baker, Marina. *Spells for Teenage Witches.* Berkeley, Calif.: Seastone, 2000.

Bartlett, John. *Bartlett's Familiar Quotations* (sixteenth edition). Boston, Mass.: Little, Brown, and Company, 1992.

Carr-Gomm, Phillip, and Stephanie Carr-Gomm. *The Druid Animal Oracle.* New York, N.Y.: Simon and Schuster, 1994.

Conway, D. J. *Dancing with Dragons.* St. Paul, Minn.: Llewellyn, 1999.

———. *Lord of Light and Shadow: The Many Faces of the God.* St. Paul, Minn.: Llewellyn, 1997.

———. *Maiden, Mother, and Crone: The Myth and Reality of the Triple Goddess.* St. Paul, Minn.: Llewellyn, 1994.

Crowley, Vivianne. *Wicca: The Old Religion in the New Millennium.* London: Thorsons Publishing, 1996.

Cunningham, Scott. *Earth, Air, Fire, and Water: More Techniques of Natural Magic.* St. Paul, Minn.: Llewellyn, 1992.

———. *Cunningham's Encyclopedia of Crystal, Gem and Metal Magic.* St. Paul, Minn.: Llewellyn, 1992.

————. *Cunningham's Encyclopedia of Magical Herbs*. St. Paul, Minn.: Llewellyn, 1985.

————. *The Truth About Witchcraft Today*. St. Paul, Minn.: Llewellyn, 1993.

Dugan, Ellen. *Garden Witchery: Magick from the Ground Up*. St. Paul, Minn.: Llewellyn, 2003.

————. "Teen Witch Survival Guide." *Llewellyn's 2002 Magical Almanac*. St. Paul, Minn.: Llewellyn, 2001.

Harvey, Andrew, and Anne Barring. *The Devine Feminine*. Berkeley, Calif.: Conari Press, 1996.

Hodson, Geoffrey. *Fairies at Work and at Play*. Wheaton, Ill.: Quest Books, 1982.

Laufer, Geraldine Adamich. *Tussie-Mussies: The Victorian Art of Expressing Yourself in the Language of Flowers*. New York: Workman Publishing Company, Inc., 1993.

Llewellyn's 2002 Magical Almanac. St. Paul, Minn.: 2001.

Manning, Al G. *Helping Yourself with White Witchcraft*. West Nyack, N.Y.: Parker Publishing Company, 1972.

Matthews, John. *The Quest for the Green Man*. Wheaton, Ill.: Quest Books, 2001.

Monaghan, Patricia. *The New Book of Goddesses and Heroines*. St. Paul, Minn.: Llewellyn, 1998.

Nahmad, Claire. *Garden Spells*. Philadelphia, Pa.: Running Press Books, 1994.

O'Rush, Claire. *The Enchanted Garden*. New York: Gramercy Books, 2000.

Ravenwolf, Silver. *Teen Witch: Wicca for a New Generation*. St. Paul, Minn.: Llewellyn, 1998.

————. *To Ride a Silver Broomstick*. St. Paul, Minn.: Llewellyn, 1993.

Skolnick, Solomon, M. *The Language of Flowers*. White Plains, N.Y.: Peter Pauper Press, Inc., 1995.

South, Malcolm. *Mythical and Fabulous Creatures*. Westport, Conn.: Greenwood Press, 1987.

Starhawk. *The Spiral Dance* (10th anniversary edition). San Francisco, Calif.: Harper Collins, 1989.

Stewart, R. J. *Celtic Gods Celtic Goddesses*. New York: Sterling Publishing, 1990.

Valiente, Doreen. *Natural Magic*. Custer, Wash.: Phoenix Publishing, 1975.

Walker, Barbara. *The Woman's Dictionary of Sacred Symbols and Objects*. New York: Harper Collins Publishers, 1988.

West, Kate. *The Real Witches' Handbook*. London: Thorsons Publishing, 2001.

Note: Bold type indicates the most important page number for the entry.

Llewellyn publishes hundreds of books on your favorite subjects!
To get these exciting books, including the ones on the following pages,
check your local bookstore or order them directly from Llewellyn.

Order Online

Visit our website at www.llewellyn.com, select your books, and order them on
our secure server.

Order by Phone

- Call toll-free within the U.S. at 1-877-NEW-WRLD (1-877-639-9753)
- Call toll-free within Canada at 1-866-NEW-WRLD (1-866-639-9753)
- We accept VISA, MasterCard, and American Express

Order by Mail

Send the full price of your order (MN residents add 7% sales tax) in U.S. funds,
plus postage & handling to:

>   Llewellyn Worldwide
>   P.O. Box 64383, Dept. 0-7387-0393-1
>   St. Paul, MN 55164-0383, U.S.A.

Postage & Handling

Standard (U.S., Mexico, & Canada). If your order is:

>   Up to $25.00, add $3.50
> $25.01–$48.99, add $4.00
> $49.00 and over, FREE STANDARD SHIPPING
>   (Continental U.S. orders ship UPS. AK, HI, PR, & P. O. Boxes
>   ship USPS 1st class. Mex. & Can. ship PMB.)

International Orders

>   *Surface Mail:* For orders of $20.00 or less, add $5 plus $1 per item
>   ordered. For orders of $20.01 and over, add $6 plus $1 per item
>   ordered.

>   *Air Mail:* For books, postage & handling is equal to the total retail
>   price of all books in the order. For non-book items, add $5 for each
>   item.

Orders are processed within 2 business days. Please allow for normal shipping time.
Postage and handling rates subject to change.

Garden Witchery

Magick from the Ground Up
(Includes a Gardening Journal)

ELLEN DUGAN

How does your magickal garden grow?

Garden Witchery is more than belladonna and wolfsbane. It's about making your own enchanted backyard with the trees, flowers, and plants found growing around you. It's about creating your own flower fascinations and spells, and it's full of common-sense information about cold hardiness zones, soil requirements, and a realistic listing of accessible magickal plants.

There may be other books on magickal gardening, but none have practical gardening advice, magickal correspondences, flower folklore, moon gardening, faerie magick, advanced witchcraft, and humorous personal anecdotes all rolled into one volume.

- This master gardener and practicing Witch will inspire gardeners of all ages and experience levels
- Design, plan, and maintain many kinds of Witch's gardens, including moon, container, shade, harvest, tree and bush, groundcover, fairy gardens, and houseplant gardens
- Learn the magickal meanings of plants from the perspective of color, scent, and the language of flowers
- Includes floral and herbal spells, faerie magick, Sabbat celebrations, and "Witch Crafts" (sachets, wreaths, charm bags)

ISBN 0-7387-0318-4
272 pp., 7½ x 7½ $16.95

Spellcraft for Teens
A Magical Guide to Writing & Casting Spells

GWINEVERE RAIN

Wiccan magick for teens written by a real teen witch

Empower, bewitch, and enchant. Written by a teen witch with her own popular website, *SpellCraft for Teens* contains fifty-five chants and incantations. In addition, it provides a twelve-step guide to casting a magick circle, an in-depth look at the moon phases, and the magical properties of colors, herbs, and charms. From finding a craft name to performing the three types of love spells, *SpellCraft for Teens* addresses issues specific to young adults, including telling parents about their interest in Wicca and dealing with gossiping classmates.

- A Wiccan teen writes a simple, step-by-step guide to following the Wiccan path and living a magical life
- An innovative guide that outlines the 11 steps to writing and casting a bewitching spell
- Contains a 12-step guide to casting a magick circle
- Provides 55 chants and incantations for 14 magical purposes

ISBN 0-7387-0225-0
160 pp., 7½ x 7½ $12.95

To order, call 1-877-NEW-WRLD
Prices subject to change without notice

Teen Witch

Wicca for a New Generation

SILVER RAVENWOLF

Teenagers and young adults comprise a growing market for books on Witchcraft and magick, yet there has never been a book written specifically for the teen seeker. Now, Silver RavenWolf, one of the most well-known Wiccans today and the mother of four young Witches, gives teens their own handbook on what it takes and what it means to be a Witch. Humorous and compassionate, *Teen Witch* gives practical advice for dealing with everyday life in a magickal way. From homework and crabby teachers to parents and dating, this book guides teens through the ups and downs of life as they move into adulthood. Spells are provided that address their specific concerns, such as the "Call Me Spell" and "The Exam Spell."

Parents will also find this book informative and useful as a discussion tool with their children. Discover the beliefs of Witchcraft, Wiccan traditions, symbols, holidays, rituals, and more.

ISBN 1-56718-725-0
288 pp., 7 x 10   **$12.95**

To order, call 1-877-NEW-WRLD

Prices subject to change without notice

Solitary Witch
The Ultimate Book of Shadows for the New Generation

SILVER RAVENWOLF

The BIG book for Pagan teens

This book has everything a Teen Witch could want and need between two covers: a magickal cookbook, encyclopedia, dictionary, and grimoire. It relates specifically to today's young adults and their concerns, yet is grounded in the magickal work of centuries past.

Information is arranged alphabetically and divided into five distinct categories: (1) Shadows of Religion and Mystery, (2) Shadows of Objects, (3) Shadows of Expertise and Proficiency, (4) Shadows of Magick and Enchantment, and (5) Shadows of Daily Life. It is organized so readers can skip over the parts they already know, or read each section in alphabetical order.

- By the author of the best-selling *Teen Witch* and mother of four teen Witches
- A jam-packed learning and resource guide for serious young Witches
- All categories are discussed in modern terms and their associated historical roots
- A training companion to *Teen Witch* and *To Ride a Silver Broomstick*

ISBN 0-7387-0319-2
608 pp., 8 x 10 $19.95

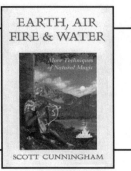

EARTH, AIR
FIRE & WATER

*More Techniques
of Natural Magic*

SCOTT CUNNINGHAM

Earth, Air, Fire & Water

More Techniques of Natural Magic

SCOTT CUNNINGHAM

A water-smoothed stone . . . the wind . . . a candle's flame . . . a pool of water. These are the age-old tools of natural magic. Born of the Earth, possessing inner power, they await only our touch and intention to bring them to life.

The four elements are the ancient powerhouses of magic. Using their energies, we can transform ourselves, our lives, and our worlds. Tap into the marvelous powers of the natural world with these rites, spells, and simple rituals that you can do easily and with a minimum of equipment. *Earth, Air, Fire & Water* includes more than seventy-five spells, rituals, and ceremonies with detailed instructions for designing your own magical spells. This book instills a sense of wonder concerning our planet and our lives; and promotes a natural, positive practice that anyone can successfully perform.

ISBN 0-87542-131-8
240 pp., 6 x 9, illus.   **$9.95**

To order, call 1-877-NEW-WRLD
Prices subject to change without notice

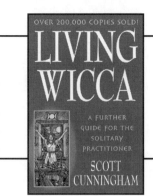

Living Wicca

A Further Guide for the Solitary Practitioner

SCOTT CUNNINGHAM

Living Wicca is the long-awaited sequel to Scott Cunningham's wildly successful *Wicca: a Guide for the Solitary Practitioner.* This book is for those who have made the conscious decision to bring their Wiccan spirituality into their everyday lives. It provides solitary practitioners with the tools and added insights that will enable them to blaze their own spiritual paths—to become their own high priests and priestesses.

Living Wicca takes a philosophical look at the questions, practices, and differences within Witchcraft. It covers the various tools of learning available to the practitioner, the importance of secrecy in one's practice, guidelines to performing ritual when ill, magical names, initiation, and the Mysteries. It discusses the benefits of daily prayer and meditation, making offerings to the gods, how to develop a prayerful attitude, and how to perform Wiccan rites when away from home or in emergency situations.

Unlike any other book on the subject, *Living Wicca* is a step-by-step guide to creating your own Wiccan tradition and personal vision of the gods, designing your personal ritual and symbols, developing your own book of shadows, and truly living your Craft.

ISBN 0-87542-184-9
208 pp., 6 x 9, illus. $12.95

To order, call 1-877-NEW-WRLD
Prices subject to change without notice

Earth Power

Techniques of Natural Magic

SCOTT CUNNINGHAM

Magick is the art of working with the forces of Nature to bring about necessary and desired changes. The forces of Nature—expressed through Earth, Air, Fire, and Water—are our "spiritual ancestors" who paved the way for our emergence from the prehistoric seas of creation. Attuning to and working with these energies in magick not only lends you the power to effect changes in your life, it also allows you to sense your own place in the larger scheme of Nature. Using the "Old Ways" enables you to live a better life and to deepen your understanding of the world. The tools and powers of magick are around you, waiting to be grasped and utilized. This book gives you the means to put magick into your life, shows you how to make and use the tools, and gives you spells for every purpose.

ISBN 0-87542-121-0

176 pp., 5¼ x 8, illus.

$9.95

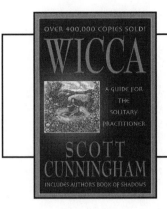

Wicca

A Guide for the Solitary Practitioner

SCOTT CUNNINGHAM

Wicca is a book of life, and how to live magically, spiritually, and wholly attuned with Nature. It is a book of sense and common sense, not only about Magick, but about religion and one of the most critical issues of today: how to achieve the much needed and wholesome relationship with our Earth. Cunningham presents Wicca as it is today: a gentle, Earth-oriented religion dedicated to the Goddess and God. This book fulfills a need for a practical guide to solitary Wicca—a need which no previous book has fulfilled.

Here is a positive, practical introduction to the religion of Wicca, designed so that any interested person can learn to practice the religion alone, anywhere in the world. It presents Wicca honestly and clearly, without the pseudo-history that permeates other books. It shows that Wicca is a vital, satisfying part of twentieth- century life.

This book presents the theory and practice of Wicca from an individual's perspective. The section on the Standing Stones Book of Shadows contains solitary rituals for the Esbats and Sabbats. This book, based on the author's nearly two decades of Wiccan practice, presents an eclectic picture of various aspects of this religion. Exercises designed to develop magical proficiency, a self-dedication ritual, herb, crystal and rune magic, as well as recipes for Sabbat feasts, are included in this excellent book.

ISBN 0-87542-118-0

240 pp., 6 x 9, illus. $9.95

To Ride a Silver Broomstick

New Generation Witchcraft

SILVER RAVENWOLF

Throughout the world there is a new generation of Witches —people practicing or wishing to practice the craft on their own, without an in-the-flesh magickal support group. *To Ride a Silver Broomstick* speaks to those people, presenting them with both the science and religion of Witchcraft, allowing them to become active participants while growing at their own pace. It is ideal for anyone: male or female, young or old, those familiar with Witchcraft, and those totally new to the subject and unsure of how to get started.

Full of the author's warmth, humor, and personal anecdotes, *To Ride a Silver Broomstick* leads you step-by-step through the various lessons with exercises and journal writing assignments. This is the complete Witchcraft 101, teaching you to celebrate the Sabbats, deal with coming out of the broom closet, choose a magickal name, visualize the Goddess and God, meditate, design a sacred space, acquire magickal tools, design and perform rituals, network, spell cast, perform color and candle magick, divination, healing, telepathy, psychometry, astral projection, and much, much more.

ISBN 0-87542-791-X
320 pp., 7 x 10, illus.   **$14.95**

The Book of Wizardry

The Apprentice's Guide to the Secrets
of the Wizards' Guild

CORNELIUS RUMSTUCKLE

The twenty-two closely guarded secrets to becoming a Wizard
Dear young Wizards in training: some people spend their whole lives trying to work magic and never get the hang of it. But now you have this book to help you. By the time you work your way through it, you will be a fully accredited Wizard.

Learn how to make a Wizard's wand and weapons, how to read your future in the Wizard's Oracle, how to switch on Wizard's Power, and how to build a Wizard's Castle in your mind. The twenty-two lessons are structured so that young readers can move up a series of grades, with the eventual aim of achieving member status in the Wizards' Guild.

- A children's (ages 10–14) interactive guide to the principles of magic
- Written by a practicing Wizard experienced in every aspect of the art
- Contains instructions for genuine energy work, meditation, visualizations, and simple magick
- Features the "Wizard's Adventure," a solo magical game based on the lessons in the book. The goal is to find the Wizards' Guild, at which point you must crack the code to become a member and receive a certificate by mail

ISBN 0-7387-0165-3
408 pp., 5³⁄₁₆ x 8, illus. $15.95

To order, call 1-877-NEW-WRLD
Prices subject to change without notice

Teen Goddess

How to Look, Love & Live Like a Goddess

CATHERINE WISHART

A girl's guide to magic, makeup, and meditation

Every girl is a goddess! When you access your goddess power, you can make your life exactly as you want it to be. This positive and hip guide to beauty and spirituality will show you how—with simple messages and tasks that will illuminate your mind, body, and soul.

Remarkable things will happen when you begin to delve into your divine beauty and listen to the inner voice of the Goddess. Find romance, ace exams, radiate confidence. Enchant everybody with your appearance and your attitude. All the glamour, strength, and magic that was available to the ancient goddesses is available to you now.

- A hip and fun girl's guide (ages 12 and up) to goddess mythology, magic, and inner and outer beauty
- Introduces fifteen powerful goddesses from different cultures
- The first book to provide "glamour recipes" for invoking the spiritual essence of a particular goddess—complete with makeup and clothes
- Provides healthy role models for girls of all shapes and sizes
- Contains meditations, affirmations, prayers, and ceremonies for each goddess

ISBN 0-7387-0392-3

384 pp., 7½ x 9⅛ $14.95

To Write to the Author

If you wish to contact the author or would like more information about this book, please write to the author in care of Llewellyn Worldwide and we will forward your request. Both the author and publisher appreciate hearing from you and learning of your enjoyment of this book and how it has helped you. Llewellyn Worldwide cannot guarantee that every letter written to the author can be answered, but all will be forwarded. Please write to:

Ellen Dugan
℅ Llewellyn Worldwide
P.O. Box 64383, Dept. 0-7387-0393-1
St. Paul, MN 55164-0383, U.S.A.

Please enclose a self-addressed stamped envelope for reply,
or $1.00 to cover costs. If outside U.S.A., enclose
international postal reply coupon.

Many of Llewellyn's authors have websites with additional information and resources. For more information, please visit our website at
http://www.llewellyn.com